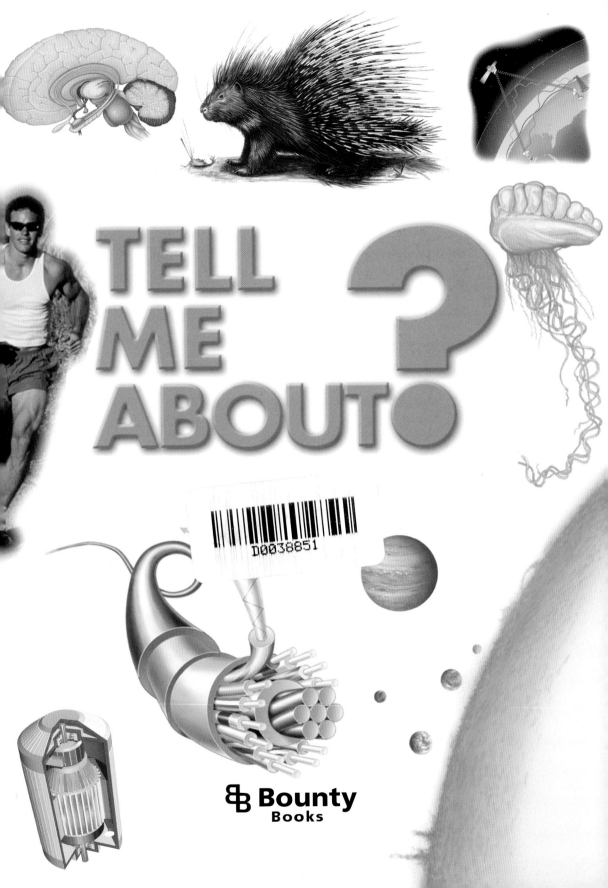

TELL ME ABOUT?

D0038851

Bounty Books

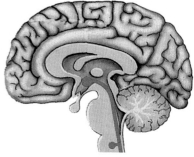

This edition first published
in 2002 by Bounty Books
a division of Octopus Publishing Group Ltd,
2-4 Heron Quays, London E14 4JP
An Hachette Livre UK Company

Copyright © 2002 Octopus Publishing Group Ltd
Reprinted 2003 (twice), 2004 (three times), 2005 (three time), 2006 (three time), 2007

ISBN-13: 978-0-753704-47-9
ISBN-10: 0-753704-47-1

Printed in China

CONTENTS

HISTORY

AND EVENTS

CONTENTS

WHO WERE THE FRANKS?

Frankish soldiers

The Franks emerged from the ruins of the Roman Empire in 476 AD as the dominant people of western Europe. Their leader, Clovis, extended his lands around the River Rhine in Germany through war and by 540 the Franks ruled most of the old Roman province of Gaul (France, named after the Franks).

The first Frankish ruling family is known as the Merovingian dynasty, after Clovis's grandfather Merovaeus. Clovis became a Christian and made Paris his capital city. Most of the Franks were peasant farmers, who lived on lands ruled by nobles. They grew food, doing the seasonal tasks of ploughing, sowing and harvesting and also had to fight for their lord when he went to war. The Frankish system of land-holding and service was the beginning of the feudal system in Europe.

Charlemagne was king of the Franks from 768 to 814, and created a vast empire. On Christmas Day in 800, the Pope crowned Charlemagne Holy Roman Emperor. After the death of Charlemagne the Frankish empire began to break up.

FACT FILE

The Frankish king Charlemagne introduced this writing, called 'Carolingian script', which was easier for people to read and write.

WHERE WAS THE GREAT CITY OF THE ANCIENT WORLD?

Babylon was the great city of the ancient world. It was the capital of the kingdom of Babylonia and of two Babylonian empires. Babylon stood on the banks of the Euphrates River near the modern city of Al Hillah in Iraq. This location helped Babylon become an important trading post. The city also served as the religious centre of Babylonia; the word 'Babylon', means *gate of the god*.

Records first mention Babylon about 2200 BCE. King Sumu-abum, the first important Babylonian ruler, founded a dynasty in 1894 BCE. The best-known king of that dynasty was Hammurabi, who ruled from 1792 to 1750 BCE and won fame for developing a wise and fair code of law.

FACT FILE

The period from 5000 to 500 BCE was an age of crucial new technologies – the wheel, metal tools and weapons were developed at this time. Coins were first used, and writing and mathematics developed. Babylonians also began to study the stars.

WHEN WAS THE SHANG DYNASTY?

The Shang dynasty was the earliest known Chinese ruling family. The dynasty governed from about 1766 BCE to about 1122 BCE. Its centre was in what is now known as the northern Henan Province. Shang society, though based on agriculture, became famous for its fine carvings and bronze work. Most Shang relics found by archaelogists come from Anyang, a city with houses, palaces, temples and elaborate tombs. The people of the Shang period used bronze to make vessels, weapons and chariot fixtures. They also carved marble and jade and wove silk. The Shang kings were superstitious and consulted 'oracle bones' before making any important decisions.

Shang food vessel

FACT FILE

The Shang writing system had more than 3,000 symbols. It appears on pieces of bone, silk and even turtle shells.

WHO WERE THE HITTITES?

Hittite charioteers

The Hittites were the earliest known inhabitants of modern-day Turkey. They began to rule the area in about 1900 BCE and during the next centuries, they conquered parts of Mesopotamia and Syria. By 1500 BCE, they had become a leading power in the Middle East. Hittite culture and language were Indo-European, but scholars do not know whether the Hittites came from Europe or from central Asia. They were the first people to use chariots in war. Hittite archers fired their arrows from these chariots, giving them a great advantage over their enemies.

One of the greatest battles of ancient times took place in about 1285 BCE at Kadesh on the Orontes River, north of Palestine. Mutwatallis, the Hittite leader, fought an indecisive battle against Egyptian forces under Rameses II, who barely escaped alive.

FACT FILE

The Hittites were the first to master iron-making, and this can be seen in their weaponry. Axe heads were made from bronze (shown here) and also iron.

9

WHO WERE THE OLMECS AND CHAVINS?

Two groups developed America's earliest civilizations – the Olmecs in Mexico and Central America, and the Chavins in Peru on the west coast of South America.

The Olmecs flourished between *c.* 1500 and 400 BCE. They made pottery, cleared the jungle to grow crops and constructed large stepped pyramids from earth. They held religious ceremonies and built temples for their gods on top of their pyramids.

The Chavins who lived in the foothills of the Andes became farmers by about 1000 BCE. They built the first towns in South America. They cut terraces into hillsides and became expert at irrigation in order to cultivate the dry land and mountain slopes.

The Olmecs

FACT FILE

In modern Peru, craftworkers carry on the traditions of their Chavin ancestors, producing bright handwoven textiles. Designs such as these have been produced in Peru for around 3,000 years.

The Chavins

WHICH GODS DID THE PERSIANS WORSHIP?

The Persians believed in gods of nature, such as the Sun and the Sky, believing they had special powers. Mithras, the god of light, can be seen here killing a bull as a sacrifice to renew life. The Persians did not build temples but worshipped on the mountaintops.

Many people followed the teachings of Zoraster (or Zarathustra). He was a prophet who lived sometime between 628 and 551 BCE and reformed the ancient religion. He taught that life was a struggle between good (light) and evil (darkness). He preached a faith based on good thoughts, words and deeds, emphasizing a supreme god called Ahura Mazda 'the wise spirit', a winged god of light. Ahura Mazda became the chief god of the Persians.

Zoraster's followers gradually spread his beliefs throughout Persia.

FACT FILE

Darius I ruled Persia from 521 to 486 BCE. He encouraged trade through the use of coins and new canals. Darius sent an army into Greece in 490 BCE, but it was defeated by Athenian forces at Marathon. Darius died in 486 BCE while preparing for new attacks on Greece.

WHAT WAS DAILY LIFE LIKE IN ANCIENT GREECE?

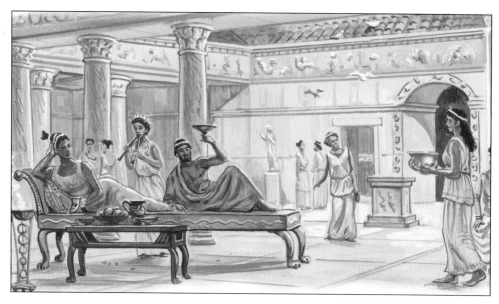

Much of what we know about how the Greeks lived comes from pictures on vases. The pictures not only show wars and stories from mythology, but also daily activities such as hunting, farming and fishing. Greek homes were built around a central courtyard, cool and airy, where the family slaves prepared food on an open fire. There was a small shrine to the household god. Many houses were built without windows in the outside walls. This design kept out both the hot sun and thieves.

People ate with their fingers while lying on wooden couches. Slaves brought in the dishes of food, while a musician played on pipes or a lyre. Men and women wore a *chiton*, a cloth square draped over the body and fastened by a pin at the shoulder.

FACT FILE

A portrait of a Greek woman on a fragment of pottery. Greek women spent most of their time around the home organizing the household.

WHY IS ALEXANDER THE GREAT REMEMBERED?

Alexander the Great (356–323 BCE) was king of the Macedonians and is remembered as one of the greatest generals in history. He conquered the Persian Empire, which stretched from the Mediterranean Sea to India and formed much of what was then considered the civilized world. Alexander's conquests furthered the spread of Greek ideas and customs in western Asia and Egypt. According to one story, as a young boy Alexander tamed the great horse Bucephalus, which was said to be too spirited and wild to control. This magnificent steed later carried Alexander into battle at Issus in 333 BCE. Alexander built a city and named it Bucephala after his horse.

FACT FILE

Alexander imposed a single system of money throughout his lands. He was keen to promote trade and commerce across the empire too.

WHO WAS ASOKA?

The Mauryan Empire was the first empire to provide a single government for almost all of India. Mauryan emperors ruled from about 324 to 185 BCE. Their empire was built around Magadha, a rich kingdom in the Ganges Valley.

This empire was ruled from about 324 to about 298 BCE by Chandragupta Maurya. His grandson Asoka was the greatest emperor of ancient India. He took government very seriously, reforming taxes, encouraging trade and farming, and building walled cities with pleasant houses and paved streets. His officials travelled the country, building roads and collecting taxes from peasant farmers in the villages.

Asoka was born a Hindu, but he became a Buddhist. He then gave up war, sickened by the slaughter he had seen during his conquest of Orissa in the southeast. Asoka made new laws and had them inscribed on stone pillars set up all across his empire.

Asoka

FACT FILE

The carved stone lions on the pillar at Sarnath have become a national emblem for India.

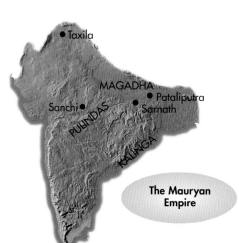

Taxila

MAGADHA

Sanchi • PULINDAS • Pataliputra
Sarnath

KALINGA

The Mauryan Empire

14

WHEN DID SETTLERS FIRST ARRIVE IN JAPAN?

People from mainland Asia had settled on the islands of Japan by 7000 BCE. The original inhabitants may have been the Ainu, about 15,000 of whom still live in Japan. The early Japanese lived by hunting and fishing. Farming began around 1000 to 500 BCE, when the Japanese began to grow rice, a skill learned from the Chinese. They also began to make metal tools and pottery using a potter's wheel. The site in Tokyo where pottery was first found gives this period of history its name – Yayoi.

The Yayoi farmers dug ditches to irrigate their rice fields. They built thatched homes and storehouses on stilts for their rice crop. Farmers lived together in villages, and each village was led by a chief who was often a woman shaman, or magician. The women shamans of Japan were extremely powerful figures.

FACT FILE

During Japan's Yayoi period, the dead were often buried inside stone tombs, like the one shown here.

WHICH GODS DID THE ANCIENT GREEKS WORSHIP?

TELL ME ABOUT : HISTORY AND EVENTS

Zeus

The Greeks believed in many different gods, chief among these were a family of supernatural beings who lived on Mount Olympus and watched over humanity. Some gods looked after the harvest; others cared for wild animals, the sea, war and so on. King of the gods was Zeus, whom the Romans called Jupiter. The first Olympic Games, which took place in 776 BCE, were held in his honour.

The Greeks believed that the universe was a sphere. The upper half was light and airy, the lower half dark and gloomy, and the Earth was a flat disc, floating between the two halves. When people died they went to the Underworld, which was ruled by Hades, the brother of Zeus. Poseidon was the Greek god of the sea, and is often shown carrying a three-pronged spear, called a trident.

Poseidon

The Greeks believed Poseidon to be the brother of Zeus, the king of the gods, and Hades, god of the Underworld. He was also associated with horses, and the Greeks thought that he was the father of the winged horse, Pegasus.

FACT FILE

The ruins of Greek and Roman temples can be seen across Europe, the Near East and North Africa. Every town had its own temple, dedicated to a protector god or goddess.

WHO WAS ALFRED THE GREAT?

FACT FILE

The Alfred jewel was found near Athelney in Somerset in 1693. It may be part of a bookmark. On it are the words 'Alfred had me made' in Latin.

Alfred the Great (849 to 899) was king of the West Saxons in southwestern England. He saved his kingdom, Wessex, from the Danish Vikings and laid the basis for the unification of England under the West Saxon monarchy. He also led a revival of learning and literature. He was such an outstanding leader in war and peace that he is the only English king known as 'the Great'.

Alfred became king in 871, after the death of his brother Ethelred. Alfred built forts and fortified towns at strategic points. He stationed his fleet along the coast as protection against further invasions from the Danes. He also issued a code of laws to restore peaceful government and encouraged the translation of famous Christian books from Latin into English.

WHO WAS THE FIRST NORMAN KING OF ENGLAND?

William I (*c*.1027–1087), known as the Conqueror, was the first Norman king of England. He took power in 1066, following his victory over the Anglo-Saxons. As king, he maintained tight control over the country's central government.

William was born at Falaise, in Normandy in northwestern France. He was the son of Robert I, Duke of Normandy, and inherited Normandy in 1035, at about the age of eight. During his youth there were many uprisings. In 1047, William put down a great rebellion at the battle of Val-es-dunes, near Caen, with the aid of his lord, King Henry I of France. From this time on William ruled Normandy with an iron hand.

William was crowned king in Westminster Abbey on Christmas Day, 1066. He took lands from those who resisted him and kept some of these lands for himself and gave the rest to his followers in return for military service. At Salisbury in 1086, he made all the landholders swear allegiance directly to him as King.

FACT FILE

A crucial battle was fought on October 14, 1066, at Senlac Hill, north of Hastings. The English, who fought on foot, resisted bravely as Norman cavalry charged their wall of shields, and archers fired showers of arrows at them. This battle is recorded in 72 scenes on the Bayeux Tapestry.

WHO WERE THE TEUTONIC KNIGHTS?

The Teutonic Knights is the name of an organization of German crusaders founded in 1190. The Teutonic Knights modelled their organization on two earlier crusading orders, the Knights Templars and the Knights Hospitallers. The crusades were part of a Christian movement to recapture the Holy Land from the Moslems, in which kings, nobles and thousands of knights, peasants and townspeople took part. The crusades were originally called armed pilgrimages, the word 'crusade' coming from the Latin word *crux*, meaning cross.

In the 13th century, the Teutonic Knights shifted their activities to central Europe, where they tried to convert and control the people of what became Prussia, Lithuania, Latvia and Estonia. Their power and influence spread throughout central and eastern Europe.

In the 14th century, the Teutonic Knights lost much of their power, and were finally overthrown by the Poles and Lithuanians.

FACT FILE

At the end of the crusades many of the knights stayed on to guard the conquered land. They were known to build fine castles.

HOW DID A SPIDER HELP ROBERT THE BRUCE?

Robert the Bruce (1274 to 1329) was a gallant Scottish king. After claiming the throne in 1306, he spent most of his reign trying to free his country from English rule. A legend is told of Bruce hiding from his enemies. He was lying on a bed in a hut, when he saw a spider trying to swing itself from one beam to another by one of its threads. It tried six times and failed. Bruce realized that he had fought the same number of battles in vain against the English. He decided that if the spider tried a seventh time and succeeded, he would also try again. The spider's seventh attempt was successful, so Bruce took heart and went forth to victory.

Within two years he had gained control of almost all of Scotland. He then advanced into England, destroying everything in his path. In 1314, the English invaded Scotland, but Bruce's forces defeated them, in a battle at Bannockburn. Edward III finally recognized Scotland's independence and the right of Bruce to the throne, as King Robert I, in 1328.

FACT FILE

Over 10,000 English soldiers were killed at the battle of Bannockburn in 1314. By 1328 Bruce had driven the English out of Scotland.

WHO WAS THE 'MAID OF ORLEANS'?

Joan of Arc (1412 to 1431) was a French nationalist heroine who became a saint of the Roman Catholic Church. She was a simple peasant girl who rescued France from defeat in one of the darkest periods of the Hundred Years' War with England. Her first great triumph was to lead a French army against the English who had laid siege to the city of Orleans. She has often been called the 'Maid of Orleans' in reference to that victory.

Jeanne d'Arc, as she is known in France, was born at Domremy, near Nancy. She was a strong and healthy child. Like most peasants at that time, she never learned to read or write. She grew up as a devout Catholic under the strong influence of her deeply religious mother. The girl called herself Jeanne la Pucelle (Joan the Maid). By the age of 13, Joan was having religious visions which persuaded her that God had chosen her to help King Charles VII of France drive the English from France. The English saw Joan as an agent of the devil, and she was burned at the stake before a large crowd in Rouen on May 30, 1431.

FACT FILE

Joan set out with her army in April 1429 to rescue Orleans from the English. At first, the French commanders hesitated to obey her. However, they soon realized that all went well when they followed her orders. Joan's forces broke the siege of Orleans in only ten days.

WHY WAS THE GREAT WALL OF CHINA BUILT?

The Great Wall of China is the longest structure ever built. Its length is about 6,400 km (4,000 miles), and it was erected entirely by hand. The wall crosses northern China between the east coast and north-central China.

Most of what is now called the Great Wall dates from the Ming dynasty (1368 to 1644). In response to the growing threat of a Mongol invasion, the Ming government began to build a fortified wall in the late 15th century. This wall included most of what remains today. Like earlier walls, it protected China from minor attacks but provided little defence against a major invasion. The wall no longer serves any defensive purpose but it attracts many visitors from around the world.

FACT FILE

Ming means bright in Chinese, and the period was important especially in the arts. Under the Ming emperors, art and literature flourished in China, notably the making of the blue and white pottery, still famous today as Ming porcelain.

WHY WERE GUILDS FORMED?

A medieval shop

FACT FILE

Each occupation, including these blacksmiths, had its own guild. The guilds fixed prices and standards of work, and made sure their members were well paid.

In the late Middle Ages people began to live in cities. After the merchants and craftsmen settled in the towns, they set up organizations called guilds. A guild protected its members against unfair business practices, established prices and wages, and settled disputes between workers and employers.

Guilds played an important part in town government. When the first guilds were organized, the towns had few laws to protect their merchants. Most laws were made and enforced by the lord who owned the land on which a town stood. As the townspeople gained power, they demanded the right to govern themselves. All workers in a trade guild had to undergo a long and hard training. The guilds soon grew rich and powerful as they were able to set the prices that all the tradesmen in the guild were allowed to charge.

WHAT DID EARLY EXPLORERS USE FOR NAVIGATION?

An astrolabe

An astrolabe is an instrument used by early astronomers and navigators to measure the angles of celestial bodies above the horizon. It consists of a metal disc mounted on a circular frame and is suspended so that it remains vertical. The disc has sights for observing a star, and the frame has a set of marks for measuring the star's elevation. Later the astrolabe was replaced by the sextant and other more accurate instruments.

People probably made rough maps even before they began to use written language some 5,500 years ago. Over the centuries, maps became more accurate as people explored the world and developed better ways to make maps. It was not until the late 15th century that European scholars agreed that the world was round. An early map of the world appeared in a 1482 edition of Ptolemy's eight-volume *Geography*.

FACT FILE

Ferdinand Magellan was a Portuguese sea captain who commanded the first expedition that sailed around the world. His voyage provided the first positive proof that the Earth is round. Many scholars consider his voyage the greatest navigational feat in history.

WHO WAS FRANCISCO PIZARRO?

In the mid -1520s, the Spanish adventurer Francisco Pizarro began to explore the west coast of South America. He had heard tales of the Inca empire and its gold and silver treasure. In about 1527, Pizarro and a few of his followers landed near the Inca city of Tumbes on Peru's north coast; they became the first white men to set foot in Peru.

Pizarro saw enough treasure at Tumbes to convince him that the legends about the Inca were true. He returned in 1532 with about 180 men, who were later joined by other Spanish troops. By the end of 1533, the Spanish had easily conquered most of Peru, including the fabulous city of Cusco, the Inca capital. In 1535, Pizarro founded Lima, which became the centre of the Spanish government in South America.

FACT FILE

By 1550 Spain ruled most of Central and South America and the West Indies. Fleets of Spanish galleons carried gold, silver, and plundered treasures across the Atlantic to Europe.

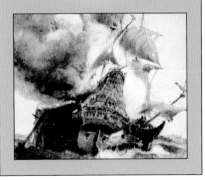

WHO WAS *DON QUIXOTE*?

Don Quixote is a novel written in two parts (1605 and 1615) by the great Spanish writer Miguel de Cervantes. It tells the story of a landowner (Quixote) who, attracted by tales of knights of old, dresses up in armour and sets out to perform heroic deeds. The first part of the novel takes Quixote from his small village in La Mancha to the forests of the Sierra Morena; he then returns to his village where he recuperates from exhaustion and various sundry injuries. The second part of the novel is more complex. This time Quixote is accompanied on his travels by his trusty servant Sancho Panza.

FACT FILE

Until the mid-19th century, when pens with steel nibs became popular, most people wrote with quill pens. The feather was trimmed to a point with a knife.

WHO BECAME 'THE MAGNIFICENT' OTTOMAN SULTAN?

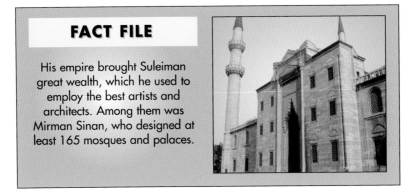

In 1520, the greatest of the Ottoman rulers came to the throne. His name was Suleiman, and he was soon to become known as 'The Magnificent' because of the splendour of his court and the might of his armies. His capital Constantinople, renamed Istanbul, was the biggest city in the world. Suleiman set out to expand his empire even further. He captured cities as far afield as Belgrade, Baghdad and Algiers, as well as Aden and the island of Rhodes. In 1526 he smashed the forces of the Hungarian king at the battle of Mohacz. Meanwhile his navy, led by the corsair Barbarossa, ruled the Mediterranean.

Suleiman was not just a fine leader and warrior, he was also a poet and a scholar. Suleiman was also known as *al-Qanuni*, 'the law-giver'. He had complete control over the daily lives of his subjects, and chose slaves from his own bodyguard to govern provinces of the empire. He reformed the legal system, so that land rents and taxes were collected properly. Even after his death in 1566, the Ottoman Empire continued to grow.

FACT FILE

His empire brought Suleiman great wealth, which he used to employ the best artists and architects. Among them was Mirman Sinan, who designed at least 165 mosques and palaces.

WHAT WAS REMBRANDT FAMOUS FOR?

Rembrandt (1606 to 1669) was a Dutch baroque artist, who ranks as one of the greatest painters in the history of Western art. His full name was Rembrandt Harmensz van Rijn. He possessed a profound understanding of human nature that was matched by a brilliant technique – not only in painting but in drawing and etching – and his work made an enormous impact on his contemporaries and influenced the style of many later artists. Rembrandt, born in Leiden on July 15, 1606, was the son of a miller. Despite the fact that he came from a family of relatively modest means, his parents took great care with his education. Rembrandt began his studies at the Latin School, and at the age of 14 he was enrolled at the Leiden University.

FACT FILE

Leonardo da Vinci was one of the great Renaissance painters. His portrait of the Mona Lisa is known throughout the world. Da Vinci was also a great inventor, recording ideas on subjects ranging from anatomy to geology. This is his painting called the Head of Leda.

WHO FORMED THE 'NEW MODEL ARMY'?

Oliver Cromwell (1599 to 1658) led the Parliamentary forces to victory in the English Civil War in the 1640s and ruled England from 1653 to 1658. He was a military genius with an iron will. Few leaders have inspired more love and respect or more fear and hatred. In the winter of 1644–1645, Cromwell led a fierce campaign to purge the high command. Cromwell's friends persuaded Parliament to establish a full-time professional army, the New Model Army, under Sir Thomas Fairfax, with Cromwell as general. The New Model Army (the Roundheads) never lost a major battle. At the Battle of Naseby, in Northamptonshire (June 14, 1645), they destroyed the king's main field army. Cromwell's men earned the nickname 'Ironsides'.

FACT FILE

The term *Roundhead* originally referred to the Parliamentary infantryman, with his hair cut short to fit his *casque* (steel helmet). By the end of the English Civil War, the armies of Parliament were superior in cavalry and infantry.

WHO WERE THE JAPANESE SHOGUNS?

Shogun was the title of the warrior rulers who led Japan from the late 12th century to the mid-19th century. The term *shogun* means great general in Japanese. The emperor of Japan first gave this title to officers sent to fight tribes in the northern frontier region in the late 8th century. In 1192, the emperor gave the title shogun to the military leader Yoritomo of the Minamoto family. Yoritomo established a *shogunate* (warrior government) in Kamakura. The Kamakura shogunate, which lasted until 1333, shared civil and military rule with the imperial court at Kyoto.

The Ashikaga family established a shogunate in the Muromachi district of Kyoto in 1338. The Ashikaga shoguns were weak and unable to maintain control. This period was marked by battles among the warrior class, called the *samurai*. In 1603, clan leader Tokugawa Ieyasu defeated his rivals and established himself as shogun of the whole country.

FACT FILE

In 1603 Ieyasu founded the most powerful shogunate in Edo (now Tokyo). In 1867 the shogun resigned and returned power to the emperor.

WHICH WAS NAPOLEON'S MOST FAMOUS BATTLE?

FACT FILE

Napoleon's first wife was Josephine, the daughter of a planter from the French West Indies. She was both intelligent and beautiful, but she and Napoleon had no children.

After years of political dispute and unrest, the French people welcomed Napoleon as their new leader in 1799. Not only was Napoleon a brilliant general, he also proved himself to be a skilful administrator. By 1812 Napoleon had created a French empire that covered almost the whole of Europe.

The Battle of Waterloo, fought on June 18, 1815, was to be his final and most famous battle. It took place at Waterloo, a small town near Brussels. His defeat by Wellington's troops was so crushing that now, when a person suffers a disastrous upset, we say the person has 'met his (or her) Waterloo'. After this defeat, Napoleon failed to gather a new army. He had no choice left but to abdicate to St Helena, where he died in 1821.

WHO GAVE THE GETTYSBURG ADDRESS?

Abraham Lincoln (1809 to 1865) was the 16th president of the United States and one of the great leaders in American history. A humane, far-sighted statesman in his lifetime, he became a legend and a folk hero after his death.

   The Gettysburg Address was a short speech that Lincoln delivered during the American Civil War at the site of the Battle of Gettysburg in Pennsylvania. He delivered the address on November 19, 1863, at ceremonies to dedicate a part of the battlefield as a cemetery for those who had lost their lives in the battle. Lincoln wrote the address to help ensure that the battle would be seen as a great Union triumph and to define for the people of the northern states the purpose in fighting the war.

FACT FILE

Abraham Lincoln was against slavery, and his election convinced the leaders of the southern states that the only option to them was to leave the Union. South Carolina was the first state to leave in 1860, soon followed by Mississippi, Florida, Alabama, Georgia and Louisiana.

WHO FOUNDED FASCISM?

Benito Mussolini (1883 to 1945) founded fascism and ruled Italy for almost 21 years, most of that time as a dictator. He dreamed of building Italy into a great empire, but instead he led his nation to defeat in World War II and was executed by his own people. In 1919, Mussolini founded the *Fasci di Combattimento*. This movement appealed to war veterans with a plan that supported government ownership of national resources and that put the interests of Italy above all others. In 1921, he transformed the *Fasci* into the National Fascist Party, adopting a more conservative scheme to gain the support of property-owning Italians.

FACT FILE

Sir Oswald Mosley formed the British Union of Fascists in the 1930s. He and his black-shirted followers were involved in riots, especially in London's East End. In World War II, Mosley was imprisoned for his pro-German views. Later, he tried to revive fascism in the United Kingdom.

WHAT WAS THE ATLANTIC CHARTER?

The Atlantic Charter expressed the peace aims of the United States and the United Kingdom for making a better future for the world after World War II. President Franklin D. Roosevelt of the United States and Winston Churchill Prime Minister of Britain adopted the declaration in August 1941 during a conference aboard ship off the coast of the Canadian province of Newfoundland. Below is a short excerpt from the Charter:

'. . . First, their countries seek no aggrandizement, territorial or other; Second, they desire to see no territorial changes that do not accord with the freely expressed wishes of the peoples concerned . . . Eighth, they believe that all the nations of the world, for realistic as well as spiritual reasons, must come to the abandonment of the use of force . . .'

FACT FILE

Representatives from 26 countries signed a document known as the 'Declaration of United Nations' on January 1, 1942. A further 21 countries later signed the same declaration.

WHAT WAS APARTHEID?

From 1948 until 1991, the South African government segregated people of different racial origin using a strict system called *apartheid*, from the Arfikaans word for separateness. Everyone was classified as white, mixed race, black or Asian, and people from the four groups were kept strictly separate: they could not live in the same areas; shop in the same shops; go to the same doctor; attend the same school or even get on the same bus. Thousands of people were imprisoned for protesting against the system. After years of international pressure, including bars on South African goods being sold abroad and sportsmen and women being banned from all international competition, the government finally repealed the last of the apartheid laws in 1991.

FACT FILE

In 1962 the United Nations General Assembly urged its members to boycott South Africa to force it to abolish apartheid, which it finally began to do in 1990.

WHO INTRODUCED PERESTROIKA AND GLASNOST?

Mikhail Sergeyevich Gorbachev was the leader of the Soviet Union from 1985 to 1991. As Soviet leader, Gorbachev gained worldwide fame for his efforts to make changes in his country and its relations with other nations. In 1990, Gorbachev received the Nobel Peace Prize for his contributions to world peace. Gorbachev made many proposals to change the Soviet political system to make it and other parts of the Soviet social system more open and democratic. He called for a reduction in the power of the Communist Party – which controlled the country – and increased power for elected bodies. His programme of economic and political reform was called *perestroika* (restructuring). His call for more openness was known as *glasnost*.

FACT FILE

The US President Ronald Reagan was a keen supporter of Gorbachev's programme of reforms in the USSR. In 1987 the two leaders signed an agreement to dismantle many kinds of nuclear weapon.

WHY IS
NELSON MANDELA FAMOUS?

Nelson Mandela is an internationally respected figure. In 1942, he joined the African National Congress (ANC), a political party that led the struggle against the injustices of white-minority rule in South Africa. He was imprisoned for conspiracy to overthrow the South African government in 1962 and remained there until 1990. Over the years, he became a symbol of the struggle against racism. He became President of the ANC in 1991 and negotiated with the government to dismantle *apartheid*. In 1994, he was elected the first black President of South Africa. Since retiring in 1999, he has used his influence to fight against injustice, racism, poverty and AIDs.

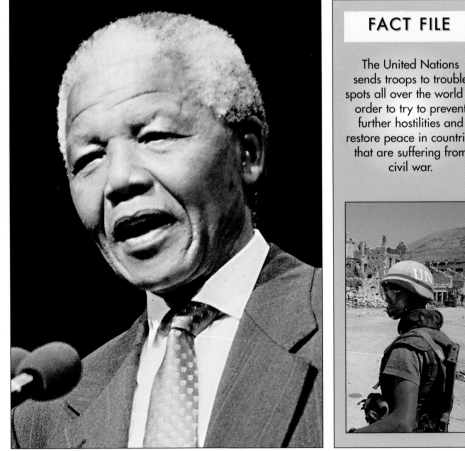

FACT FILE

The United Nations sends troops to trouble spots all over the world in order to try to prevent further hostilities and restore peace in countries that are suffering from civil war.

THE ANIMAL

KINGDOM

CONTENTS

· ·

WHAT IS THE SKUNK'S DEFENCE MECHANISM?

A skunk

A skunk is a small furry animal with distinctive black and white markings. It is known for the foul-smelling liquid which it sprays when frightened or in danger. The smell remains for days on whatever has been sprayed.

The sprayed liquid, called musk, comes from a pair of glands near the base of the skunk's tail. The animal can spray accurately as far as 4 m (12 feet). Before it sprays, it issues a warning by stamping its front feet and by hissing or growling. The spray is so strong that it has a suffocating effect, which means it makes it hard to breathe when you are near it. And if the spray gets into the eyes, it can cause temporary blindness.

FACT FILE

Skunks are omnivorous and eat insects, small vertebrates, eggs, crustaceans, fruits, seeds and some carrion. They search for their food by digging in the ground and rooting around logs, and tree stumps.

DOES AN OSTRICH REALLY BURY ITS HEAD IN THE SAND?

The ostrich is a rather strange bird, and there are many interesting and peculiar things about it, but it does not hide its head in the sand! What may have given people this idea is that when an ostrich is frightened, it will sometimes drop to the ground, stretch out its neck, and lie still and watch intently. But when the danger comes closer, the ostrich does just what other animals do – it takes off and runs. When the ostrich is exhausted and cannot run any further, or if it must defend its nest, it kicks with its powerful legs.

FACT FILE

Although the ostrich cannot fly, it makes up for this by its ability to run at high speed. It runs faster than any other bird in the world, and can travel as fast as 50 miles an hour, maintaining this speed for at least half a mile.

WHY DO MOSQUITO BITES ITCH?

Only female mosquitoes bite and only the females of a few species attack human beings and animals. Mosquitoes do not really bite because they cannot open their jaws. When a mosquito 'bites' it stabs through the victim's skin with six needlelike parts called *stylets* which form the middle of the *proboscis*. The stylets are covered and protected by the insect's lower lip, called the *labium*. As the stylets enter the skin, the labium bends and slides upwards out of the way. Then saliva flows into the wound through channels formed by the stylets. The mosquito can easily sip the blood because the saliva keeps it from clotting. Most people are allergic to the saliva, and an itchy welt called a 'mosquito bite' forms on the skin.

FACT FILE

A mosquito is an insect that spreads some of the most serious diseases to people and animals. Some mosquitoes carry the germs that cause such deadly diseases as encephalitis, malaria, filariasis and yellow fever.

WHY DO MOTHS EAT WOOL?

There is a moth known as 'the clothes moth' and most people blame it for making moth holes in our clothes. But it isn't the moth that does the damage at all. The moth never eats; it lives only to produce its eggs and then it dies. It is when the young moth is in the caterpillar stage that all the damage is done. The moth lays its eggs on woollen fabrics and in about a week the eggs hatch into caterpillars. The caterpillar then makes a little tubular case out of the wool, and lines this case with silk. There it lives as a caterpillar until it is ready to emerge as a moth. So you see that the problem of protecting clothes against moths is to make sure that moths have no chance of laying eggs on clothes.

Eyed hawk moth

FACT FILE

When at rest, eyed hawk moths resemble a dead leaf. If alarmed, they open their forewings to reveal striking eye markings on the hind wings. This is likely to scare predators such as birds.

Death's head hawk moth

Poplar hawk moth

CAN ANIMALS UNDERSTAND ONE ANOTHER?

Howler monkeys

FACT FILE

Otters use a variety of sounds to communicate among themselves. All species have a warning growl. In addition, otters use various kinds of chirps, chuckles, screams, and squeals to express their feelings to other otters.

Although animals cannot actually talk to one another, they have a means of communicating by using certain signs and sounds. Humans have expressions to indicate anger, a shrug of the shoulder to indicate indifference, nodding and shaking the head, gestures with hands, and so on. Many animals make noises and signs to do the same thing. For example, when a mother hen makes a loud noise or crouches down, all her chicks understand this as a warning of imminent danger. Howler monkeys actually do howl to defend their territory, and their howling acts as a warning as the sound carries through the Venezuelan forests. Animals can also communicate by using smell.

WHY DO PEACOCKS HAVE SUCH BEAUTIFUL TAILS?

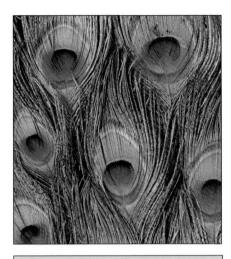

FACT FILE

In ancient times, the peacock was carried to all parts of the world as a great treasure. Both the Greeks and Romans considered it a sacred bird.

We often hear the expressions 'as proud as a peacock' or 'vain as a peacock'; this is because the peacock seems to take great pleasure in displaying its beautiful feathers. There are some interesting things about this gorgeous display, which is done solely by the male to attract a female bird. The female, the peahen, does not have these beautiful feathers. The male peacock has a metallic greenish-blue neck and breast, purplish-blue underparts, and a long train of greenish feathers brilliantly marked with bold spots that look like eyes. These feathers grow from the back and not the tail. During courtship, the male bird spreads the train into a stunning fan as he parades slowly in front of the female. In fact, the male goes through a dance as he tries to convince the peahen that he is a very handsome fellow indeed.

HOW DO BIRDS SWIM UNDERWATER?

Kingfisher

Gannet

Coot

Birds like the gannet and coot can swim underwater as well as on the surface. Most underwater swimmers, such as cormorants, dive from a floating position on the surface. They give a strong kick, point their heads downward and dive. Some fish-eating birds, including kingfishers and terns, dive into the water from high in the air. They do not swim but bob to the surface and fly away. Grebes can control the depth at which they swim by regulating the amount of air in their lungs and trapped in their plumage. By slowly letting out some air, they can gradually submerge themselves until only their heads show above the surface, like a periscope, thus they can swim along unnoticed and watch for enemies at the same time.

FACT FILE

The spoonbill is a long-legged wading bird that has a spoon-shaped bill. The bird swings its bill from side to side in the water to search for food.

WHAT ARE ARMY ANTS?

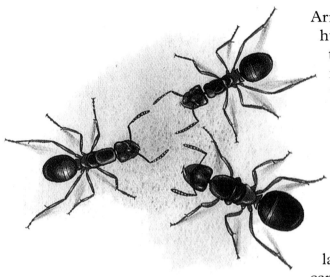

Army ants are fierce hunters. Most species travel across the land in narrow columns, while others hunt underground, moving through tunnels in the soil. Army ants prey chiefly on other insects and spiders. In some cases, they also kill and eat larger animals that cannot escape quickly.

Most army ant colonies have between 10,000 to several million members. Army ants that live above ground do not build permanent nests. When they rest, they cling together in a large cluster. They may hang from the branch of a tree or roost inside a hollow log or other suitable place. The queen and her brood nest within the large cluster of bodies.

Some kinds of army ant hunt for a few weeks and then rest for a few weeks. During the hunting periods, they may nest at a different site every night. During the resting periods, they stay in one place, and the queen lays hundreds or thousands of eggs.

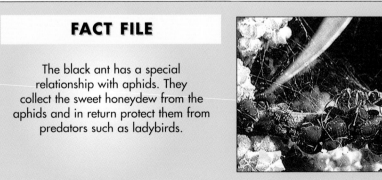

FACT FILE

The black ant has a special relationship with aphids. They collect the sweet honeydew from the aphids and in return protect them from predators such as ladybirds.

DOES A STARFISH HAVE EYES?

A starfish, also called a sea star, is a spiny-skinned sea animal that has thick, armlike extensions on its body. Most species of starfish have five such 'arms' and look rather like five-pointed stars. Some species have as many as 40 arms or more. Starfish are found in all the world's oceans.

The starfish's body has a central disc and arms. Its mouth, in the middle of the underside of the central disc, leads directly into a large, baglike stomach. On the outside of the body, a groove extends from the mouth to the tip of each arm. Rows of slender tube feet line these grooves. The tube feet often have suction discs on the ends. The animal uses the tube feet to crawl and find food. The starfish senses light with a small eye at the tip of each arm. It does not have a brain, but has nerve cords suspended in the grooves of its arms.

FACT FILE

Many starfish can drop an arm as a defence reaction. They can then grow a new arm to replace the old one.

WHY DO FLIES RUB THEIR LEGS TOGETHER?

When you see a fly rubbing its legs together, it is cleaning itself, and scraping off some of the material that has gathered there. A fly is an insect with a pair of well-developed wings. The common housefly is one of the best-known kinds of flies; a scavenger, it does not bite living animals but is dangerous because it carries bacteria that cause many serious diseases such as typhoid fever, cholera and dysentery. The housefly feeds by depositing a drop of digestive liquid on its food, which may be food that has been left uncovered.

Disease can also be transmitted on the fly's sticky foot pads and hairy body.

Common housefly

Greenbottle

Flesh fly

FACT FILE

Flies have an extremely keen sense of smell. A fungus called the stinkhorn contains a sticky, foul-smelling jelly which attracts flies. The flies eat the jelly and spread the spores when they fly away.

WHAT IS A VAMPIRE BAT?

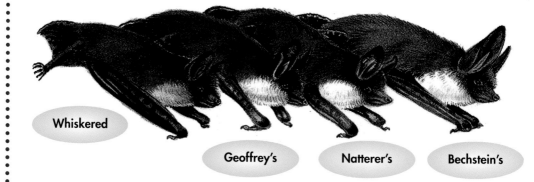

Whiskered

Geoffrey's

Natterer's

Bechstein's

The vampire bat is the name given to several different bats, particularly to certain bats in Central America and tropical America, which attack horses, cattle, birds and other warm-blooded animals and drink their blood. The best known is the common vampire bat, a small reddish-brown animal about 8 cm (3 inches) long. It has very sharp, triangular-shaped front teeth, which cut like a razor. Its oesophagus is short and narrow, and allows nothing but fluids to pass. Weird stories have been told about the viciousness of these mammals. Their peculiar name comes from the superstitious legends about the vampire, an imaginary being that sucked the blood from human beings.

FACT FILE

Many species of bats live in colonies that may have thousands or even millions of members. Others live alone or in small groups. Most bats spend the day sleeping in their roost.

Long-eared bat

ARE A DONKEY AND A JACKASS THE SAME?

A jackass is the name for a male donkey. A female donkey is called a jennet. Donkey is the name of the domesticated ass. The wild ass of northern and north-eastern Africa is the ancestor of the donkey. This wild ass looks like a zebra but with no stripes, except occasionally on the legs. It stands about 1.2 m (4 feet) high at the shoulders, and its coat is grey, with a darker line running along its back. Other characteristics of the species are long ears, small feet and long hair at the end of the tail. Thousands of years ago, people tamed the African wild ass and reared it for their own use. The domesticated donkey is most common in southern Asia, southern Europe and northern Africa.

FACT FILE

If a male donkey is mated with a mare (female horse), the animal that is born is a mule. Mules are hardy and resist disease well. Unfortunately, mules do not have offspring of their own, except in extremely rare cases. All male mules and most female mules are sterile.

WHY DOES A CAMEL HAVE A HUMP?

The camel is called 'the ship of the desert' and there is a good reason for this. Just as a ship is constructed to deal with all the problems that arise from being in the water, so a camel is built to live and travel and survive in the desert. Where other animals would die from lack of food and water, the camel can survive as it carries its food and water with it. For days before it starts on a journey, a camel does nothing but eat and drink. It eats so much that a hump of fat, weighing as much as 45 kg (100 lb), rises on its back. So, the camel's hump is a storage place for fat, which the camel's body will use during the journey. The camel also has flask-shaped bags which line the walls of its stomach, and this is where it stores water. With these provisions, a camel is able to travel several days between water holes without drinking.

FACT FILE

There are two kinds of camel: (1) the Arabian camel, also called the dromedary, which has one hump, and (2) the Bactrian camel, which has two humps.

WHAT IS THE DIFFERENCE BETWEEN RABBITS AND HARES?

Rabbit

Hares and rabbits are rodents, which means they have long, sharp front teeth. Their hindlegs are longer than their forelegs, so that they actually run faster uphill than downhill. When they are pursued, they resort to clever tricks. One is to crisscross their tracks and the other is to take huge leaps in order to break the scent. They can also signal danger to each other by thumping the ground with their hind feet.

Yet there are many differences between hares and rabbits. Hares are larger and their feet and ears are longer. Hares do not dig burrows or live in groups, as rabbits do. Hares are born open-eyed and furry, while rabbits are born blind and hairless. Hares and rabbits never mate.

A hare

FACT FILE

Hares court and mate in spring. During courtship, they often jump and twist in the air. This may explain the phrase 'mad as a March hare'.

WHAT IS A GUINEA PIG?

Guinea pigs are not really pigs. They are rodents, like rabbits, rats and mice. Guinea pigs measure from 25 to 36 cm (10 to 14 inches) long and weigh about 0.5 kg (1 lb). They have a large head, small ears and short legs. Most guinea pigs that live in their natural surroundings have long, coarse, brown or grey fur. Guinea pigs bred by animal breeders may have long or short fur of varying texture, and can be any combination of black, brown, red or white. Most kinds of wild guinea pigs live in groups of from 5 to 10 animals. They make their home on grassy plains and the edges of forests and in marshes and rocky areas. Guinea pigs dig burrows in soil or among rocks and stay there during the day. Occasionally they take over burrows abandoned by other animals. They are mainly active at night, when they feed on plants. They are timid and utter loud whistlelike squeals when frightened.

FACT FILE

The capybara is a relative of the guinea pig and is the largest of all rodents. It has webbed toes and swims well. It grazes near lakes and rivers, and plunges into the water at any sign of danger.

DOES A COW REALLY HAVE FOUR STOMACHS?

The answer to this question is no – cattle have one stomach with four compartments. This kind of stomach enables them to bring swallowed food back into their mouth to be chewed and swallowed again; this is known as chewing the cud. Animals with such stomachs are called ruminants. The compartments are the *rumen*, the *reticulum*, the *omasum* and the *abomasum*. Each cavity helps digest food with the aid of numerous micro-organisms, such as bacteria and yeasts that live in the stomach. The fourth cavity is the 'true stomach', which functions in the same way as the stomach in human beings and other mammals that are not ruminants.

WHY DO DEER SHED THEIR ANTLERS?

Deer are the only animals with bones called antlers on their heads. Antlers are part of a deer's skull. The antlers' hard, bony structure and sharp points make them extremely dangerous weapons. Male deer use them chiefly to fight for mates or for leadership of a herd. Deer that live in mild or cold climates shed their antlers each winter and begin to grow a new set in late spring. Deer in warmer climates may lose their antlers and grow new ones at other times of the year. New antlers are soft and tender and grow rapidly. A thin layer of skin covers the antlers which contains blood vessels that stimulate growth. The skin layer is called velvet because it has short, fine hairs that give it the soft appearance of velvet. As the antlers reach full size, the velvet dries and the deer scrapes it off on the ground or against trees or bushes.

FACT FILE

All antlers have branches that end in tines. They usually have five to six tines on each side, getting larger until the stag is in its teens. This specimen has 42 tines!

Red deer

HOW DO WHALES BREATHE?

Whales take in air less frequently than land mammals, and they can hold their breath for extraordinarily long periods during their dives. Although their lung capacity is no greater than that of land mammals of equivalent size, whales take deeper breaths and extract more oxygen from the air they breathe. Unlike the seal, which exhales before diving, a whale's lungs are still partially inflated. The whale's nostrils are modified to form a blowhole at the top of the head. The skin immediately surrounding the blowhole has many specialized nerve endings, which are very sensitive to the change as the blowhole breaks the water. The whale often breathes in and out again very rapidly, in the fraction of a second that the blowhole is above the surface. The blowhole is closed when the animal is submerged. When a whale surfaces and exhales, a spout of water or 'blow' can be seen.

FACT FILE

Baleen whales have two blowholes in the top of their head, whilst the toothed whales only have a single one. The 'blow' is caused by condensation from the warm, moist air that is exhaled, not from seawater trapped in the blowhole, as was once believed.

HOW DOES A KINGFISHER CATCH ITS FOOD?

The kingfisher is the name of a large family of birds found all over the world; they have large heads and long, heavy, pointed bills, short legs and short stubby tails. Their outer and middle toes are joined together by strong membranes.

The kingfisher may spend long hours sitting on a branch beside a lake or stream watching for the small fish that swim near the surface. Then, sometimes hovering for a moment in midair, the bird dives after a fish. Kingfishers usually seize their food, but occasionally they spear fish with their long bills. They then toss the fish into the air, catch it and swallow it headfirst. Kingfishers also eat crayfish, frogs, tadpoles, salamanders and insects.

FACT FILE

Kingfishers burrow in the steep walls of river banks or sandbanks. They dig a tunnel from 1.2 to 4.6 m (4 to 15 feet) long with a larger hollow at the end where they build a nest of fish bones and scales.

WHAT MAKES A MOLEHILL?

A mole is a small, heavy-bodied mammal that lives underground. It is a fast, tireless digger and has a narrow, pointed nose, a wedge-shaped head and large forelegs.

Its front paws, which turn outward, have long, broad nails. The forelegs work like shovels, scooping out the earth. The mole's hind legs are short and powerful. The animal is almost blind, with tiny eyes that are shaded by overhanging fur or skin. A mole does not have external ears, but it hears well.

A mole's home can be recognized by a cone-shaped mound of earth above it. This mound is much larger than the slightly raised roofs of the tunnels the animal makes when digging for food. Moles mainly eat worms and insects. Their digging often spoils gardens and fields.

FACT FILE

Breeding hills are very large and contain a nest of leaves and grasses. Moles are born naked, but they start to grow fur at the age of two weeks. They leave the nest after five weeks.

WHAT ARE CURLEWS AND GODWITS?

Black-tailed Godwit

Curlew

Curlews and godwits are both long-billed wading birds. The curlew is related to the sandpiper and the snipe. It is found throughout the Americas, from Patagonia, in the far south of South America, to the Arctic in North America. It also lives in Europe and Asia. Curlews have long, slender bills which curve downward. Although they are wading birds, they nest on dry ground, often far from water. It gets its name from its slender bill, which it uses to catch small crabs, shellfish, snails, worms and beetles.

A godwit's bill curves slightly upward. These birds have greyish or brownish feathers marked with spots and streaks. Godwits nest in marshes or grassy areas in northern Europe, Canada and the northern part of the United States.

FACT FILE

An avocet is another wading bird with a long, curved bill. The avocet feeds by scraping its bill along the bottom of shallow pools of water. In this way it collects small water animals, which it eats. It also eats other food that floats on or in the water.

WHAT IS A MUTE SWAN?

FACT FILE

Swans nest along the shores of marshes and ponds in the summer. They move to large lakes in the winter. Swans feed mainly on underwater plants, but because of their long necks they can graze in deeper water than ducks.

A swan is a water bird closely related to ducks and geese. Swans have a flattened bill, a long neck, water-repellent feathers, long, pointed wings, a short tail, short legs and webbed feet. A mute swan is the most common northern species. It is native to northern Europe and Asia, but it also lives in parks throughout the world. The mute swan is quieter than other swans, but it still hisses loudly when angry. The bill of the mute swan is orange with a black knob at the base. Mute swans point their bills downwards, curving their necks in a slight S-shape.

HOW DOES A FLAMINGO FEED?

A flamingo is a bird known for its long, stilt-like legs, curved bill and long neck. When they feed, flamingos dip their heads under the water and swing them to and fro, sifting through the water as

they walk. The edges of their bills have tiny, narrow crossways plates called *lamellae*. Their large, fleshy tongues pressing against the inside of the bill strains the water through the lamellae, leaving behind the small invertebrates and the vegetable matter upon which these birds feed. Flamingos live in many parts of the world and live near lakes, marshes and seas. They live in colonies, some of which have thousands of members. Flamingos only mate once a year, building a nest that consists of a mound of mud. Most of the females lay a single egg in a shallow hole at the top of the nest, and the parents take turns sitting on the egg to keep it warm.

FACT FILE

Wild flamingos once lived in Florida, but people killed them for their beautiful feathers. The flamingo's feathers vary from bright red to pale pink. For example, flamingos of the Caribbean area have coral-red feathers, and South American flamingos have pinkish-white feathers.

Golden eagle

HOW DID THE GOLDEN EAGLE GET ITS NAME?

The golden eagle is North America's largest predatory bird. The plumage of an adult eagle is mainly brown, darkening toward the wings, while the tail is greyish-brown. The feathers at the head and nape of its neck are golden brown, hence its name.

The Golden Eagle is a supreme flier. Using the rising air on the sides of their mountain habitat, they rise and spiral high into the air, covering vast areas of ground. They can ride air currents between ridges, and glide down at speeds of up to 190 kph (120 mph), then swoop up gracefully to their next landing point. This bird's flight is very graceful when moving slowly in still air, or even when battling against near hurricane force headwinds. Occasionally, they dive vertically onto their prey, and at times their speed is said to rival that of the fastest falcons.

FACT FILE

The buzzard is quite common in many areas of Britain, and often perches on wires or telegraph poles, something an eagle would never do. A buzzard can also be seen circling above its nesting territories.

WHAT IS NATURAL SELECTION?

Natural selection is a process that is also known as 'survival of the fittest'. Every time an animal or plant reproduces, tiny changes in the genes make the offspring slightly different from its parent. Sometimes these changes can make the offspring more successful than its parents. For example, a young giraffe with a longer neck than normal can graze higher in the trees than other giraffes, and so has access to more food. As a result it will become healthier and stronger, and will be more likely to breed successfully, passing its new genes for longer necks to its offspring. Other genes could be damaging, so the animals carrying them will be less successful and may eventually die out. The theory of natural selection is based on the great variation found among even closely related individuals. In most cases, no two members of a species are exactly alike. Each has a unique combination of such traits as size, appearance and ability to withstand cold or other harsh conditions.

FACT FILE

In 1858, Charles Darwin and another British naturalist, Alfred R. Wallace, presented similar theories of natural selection. Many biologists rejected the idea at first.

64

WHICH MAMMALS MIGRATE?

Caribou

Caribou are migratory animals. They live in herds in the cold northern regions, feeding on lichen. Each year, when snows bury their food supply, they migrate south to warmer regions, returning north when the snows thaw.

Barren-ground caribou spend the summer in the Arctic tundra and the winter in the evergreen forests south of the tundra. They may be found from western Alaska to western Greenland. In the western part of their range, they live in large herds, and roam for days at a time. They do not overgraze their territory because they keep moving from place to place. In summer, they eat mostly grass and the leaves of various shrubs, while in winter, they live mainly on lichens.

FACT FILE

The lemming is a plump little animal related to the mouse. When overcrowding of their habitat and scarcity of food occurs, they are forced to migrate. Every few years, according to legend, great numbers of lemmings march to the sea and drown themselves.

HOW IS AN OTTER ADAPTED FOR DIVING UNDERWATER?

The otter is a member of the weasel family. Otters live close to water and spend much of their time in it. Expert swimmers and divers, they can stay underwater for three or four minutes. They do, however, move awkwardly on land. An otter has a small, flat head, a long, thick neck and a thick tail that narrows to a point. Special muscles enable the animal to close its ears and nostrils tightly to keep out water. Elastic webbing grows between the otter's toes. In most species, the webbing is extensive enough to help the animals swim swiftly. Otters have long, coarse, guard hairs that cover and protect their short, thick underfur. This underfur traps air and keeps the otter's skin dry, and a layer of fat under the skin insulates the otter from the cold.

FACT FILE

The weasel has a long, slender body and short limbs. They are very alert, frequently sitting upright to look around and smell the air for prey. They chatter very loudly and give off a strong scent if they become frightened.

IS IT TRUE MALE SEAHORSES BECOME MOTHERS?

The seahorse is a small fish that is so named because its head resembles that of a tiny horse. We are accustomed to the idea that it is always the female that bear the offspring, but in seahorses it is the reverse. The female seahorse, when she lays her eggs, puts them into the broad pouch beneath the tail of the male. When the young have hatched and are ready to leave the pouch, the mouth of the pouch opens wide. The male alternately bends and straightens his body in convulsive jerks and finally a baby seahorse is shot out. After each birth the male rests, and when all the babies are born he shows signs of extreme exhaustion.

FACT FILE

The seahorse has been described as having the head of a horse, the tail of a monkey, the pouch of a kangaroo, the hard outer skeleton of an insect and the independently moving eyes of a chameleon.

IS THE CHIMPANZEE A MONKEY?

The chimpanzee is a monkey, but it is a special kind of monkey. It is the most intelligent one of all. The chimpanzee is an African ape that shares many characteristics with human beings. Chimpanzees are intelligent, playful, curious and easy to train. Scientific evidence suggests that chimpanzees and their closest relatives, the bonobos or pygmy chimpanzees, are more closely related to humans than any other animal. Chimpanzees are also related to gorillas, orangutans and gibbons.

The chimpanzee lives in tropical Africa from Lake Victoria in the east to Gambia in the west. Members of this species differ sufficiently so that scientists divide them into three subspecies. They are the central chimpanzee, the eastern or long-haired chimpanzee, and the western chimpanzee.

FACT FILE

The gibbon is an endangered species. The destruction of their forest homes and the capture of young animals for food or for sale as pets threaten these animals with extinction.

HOW DOES A CHAMELEON CHANGE ITS APPEARANCE?

The chameleon is a type of lizard. There are about 85 species and most of them live in the forests of Africa and Madagascar. Chameleons are known for their ability to change their appearance, but many other kinds of lizards also have this ability. A chameleon may be green, yellow or white one minute, and the next minute it may be brown or black. Chameleons may also become spotted or blotched. Many people believe chameleons change to blend with their surroundings, but the changes actually occur in response to variations in light or temperature, or as the result of fright or some other reaction to the environment. The chameleon's appearance is controlled by body chemicals called hormones, which affect pigments in the skin.

FACT FILE

Chameleons living in trees have a long, sticky tongue with which they capture their prey. The tongue, which may be as long as their entire body, is controlled by powerful muscles in the throat. It shoots out so rapidly that the human eye can hardly see it.

WHAT IS A PANGOLIN?

A pangolin is a species of animal that resembles the anteater and the armadillo. Pangolins live in southeastern Asia, Indonesia and parts of Africa south of the Sahara. Like anteaters, pangolins are toothless and have long, narrow snouts, long tails and sticky, rope-like tongues that they can thrust far out to catch the ants on which they feed. Pangolins have coats of mail formed by overlapping horny scales, instead of the coarse hair of anteaters. These scales are various shades of brown.

Pangolins vary in length from 0.9 to 1.5 m (3 to 5 feet), depending on the species. All pangolins have large, strong claws on their forefeet, which they use to rip open the nests of ants and termites. Pangolins can roll themselves into tight balls so heavily armoured that few enemies can harm them.

FACT FILE

Although the Chinese pangolin climbs with agility it feeds mainly on the ground, digging for termites with its strongly clawed feet.

CAN SQUIRRELS REALLY FLY?

There is a squirrel that lives in southern Asia that can actually fly. The flying squirrel has folds of skin between its front and back legs which enable it to glide long distances. The giant flying squirrel has a distinctive, thickly-haired flying membrane that stretches from its wrists to its hind legs and is further enlarged by a fold of skin between the base of the tail and the hind legs. This membrane is composed of sheets of muscles that can be tensed or relaxed, enabling the animal to control the direction of the glide. There is also a large spur on the edge of this membrane that helps to support it. Flying squirrels are nocturnal – which means they sleep during the day and become active at night.

FACT FILE

Ground squirrels are compact, short-tailed, burrowing rodents that are especially abundant in open country, such as grasslands and tundra. The most common ground squirrels found in North America are the small, striped or spotted rodents that are actually known as ground squirrels.

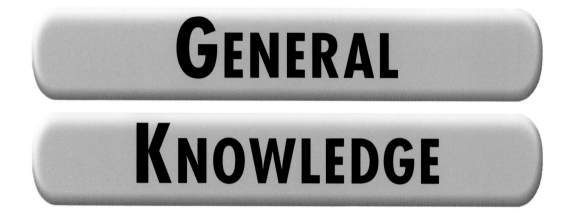

GENERAL KNOWLEDGE

CONTENTS

WHAT IS CAFFEINE?

Caffeine is found in a variety of plants, including the leaves of the tea bush and the beans of the coffee and cocoa plants. In the small amounts found in tea, coffee, colas and some medicines such as cold and flu remedies, it speeds up the heart rate and blood circulation and does no harm to most people. However, in larger doses, its stimulant effect can cause nervousness, loss of concentration and insomnia (inability to sleep), which is why people who drink lots of coffee or tea are advised to cut down. The purified chemical is colourless and odourless, and has a slightly bitter taste. As well as some over-the-counter remedies, it is also used in some treatments for heart and nerve disorders.

Picking coffee beans

FACT FILE

Cocoa pods are large and heavy. They grow on the trunk of the cacao tree or on its branches. The beans supply not only chocolate and cocoa, but also cocoa butter, which is used in sweets and medicines.

WHAT WAS THE FIRST TYPE OF SHOE?

Primitive people often had to walk long distances to find food, so they would have needed to protect their feet from rocks, hot sand, cold ice or the thorns of plants. The earliest shoes were probaby a simple type of sandal, with soles made of hide, bark, wood or woven grass which were bound to the feet and ankles with hide. The earliest known shoe that has been found by archaeologists is a slipper found in Oregon in the north-western United States and is thought to be 10,000 years old.

Ötzi the Iceman, who died in the Alps about 5,000 years ago and was found in 1991, was wearing shoes with bearskin soles, deerskin insteps and uppers made of tanned chamois or cowskin and bark. They were stuffed with grass for extra warmth.

The ancient Minoans also wore footwear: a fresco at Knossos on Crete (c. 1500 BC) shows two athletes with what look like shoes and shin guards.

Some ancient Egyptians wore sandals with leather or papyrus soles bound to their feet with two straps. Tutankhamun (d. c. 1323 BC) had several pairs in his tomb.

FACT FILE

An animal's foot has no need for shoes. It has been specially designed with a tough leathery sole to protect it.

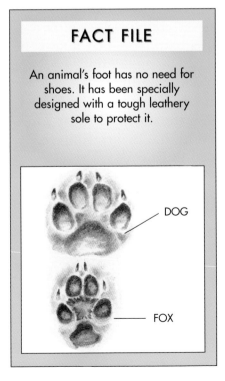

DOG

FOX

WHAT IS ETYMOLOGY?

Chinese

Hieroglyphics

Etymology is a branch of linguistics, the study of language, concerned with the origin, meaning and development of words. The word etymology (like many other scientific words) comes from Greek: *etymon* means 'true' and *logos* means 'word'. A large number of words in English are derived from Latin, often through the medieval French spoken by the ruling classes after the Norman Conquest of 1066. However, many other words reflect the earlier history of Britain: as well as words that can be traced back to Old English, Welsh is thought to be related to other Celtic languages; there are more Scandinavian-based words derived from the Vikings in the areas they conquered in the north and east and more Anglo-Saxon words in the south. With the British Empire, words from all over the world were added to English.

FACT FILE

Noah Webster (1758–1843) was born in Connecticut, USA. In 1806 Webster published *A Compendious Dictionary of the English Language*, the first truly American dictionary.

HOW ARE CRAYONS MADE?

FACT FILE

Limestone was built up under the sea over millions of years from the shells of tiny creatures called *formanifera*, which settled on the sea floor after they died and built up into a layer miles thick.

Crayons today are made from clay – a fine-grained, heavy soil – the same material as is used for making many pots. The clay is mixed with a pigment, to give it colour, and wax to prevent it drying out. Hundreds of colours are now available.

Before wax crayons were made, the most popular form were called chalks. White chalk was made from the stone of the same name (a form of limestone), black chalk from shale and red chalk from red ochre. The stone was ground, mixed with a liquid to bind it together and then dried into sticks. Pastels, which can come in many colours, are mixed with gum rather than wax or water.

WHERE WAS THE FIRST SKYSCRAPER?

The first 'skyscraper' mentioned in writing was the Tower of Babel, which is described in the Bible (Genesis), built by the descendents of Noah on the plain of Shinar in Babylonia in order to reach God. Some people think this may be a reference to a 7-storey ziggurat in Babylon.

In the Middle Ages in Europe, architects built tall towers and spires on their cathedrals for the same reason. The tallest in England is at Salisbury, finished in 1320, which rises to a total of 123 m (404 feet) above ground level.

In the 19th century, architects, especially in New York, competed to build the tallest skyscraper. One architect went so far as to conceal the top part of his building until the last minute to fool his rivals.

FACT FILE

In 1889 the Eiffel Tower in Paris was the world's tallest structure rising 300 m (984 feet) above the city.

HOW DID THE IDEA OF SANTA CLAUS ORIGINATE?

Santa Claus, or Father Christmas, has his origins in the 4th century AD. St Nicholas was Bishop of Myra in southern Turkey, and among his good deeds he gave bags of gold to three poor girls so they could marry. This is why he is particularly associated with giving gifts to children.

In some countries in northern Europe, children were given presents on December 5th, the eve of St Nicholas's Day. When Dutch migrants arrived in New York, this was mixed with the Scandinavian tradition of giving children a lump of coal or a gift according to whether they had been naughty or nice. The Dutch name San Nicholaas changed to Sankt Klaus and eventually to Santa Klaus.

In different countries gifts were given on other days: Christmas Day itself or January 6th to commemorate the gifts of the biblical Three Kings. Eventually all three traditions became mixed up and presents are now mostly given around December 25th.

FACT FILE

In England we moved the date of Santa's arrival to Christmas Eve. Gradually his red costume, the reindeer, and his home at the North Pole became part of the tradition.

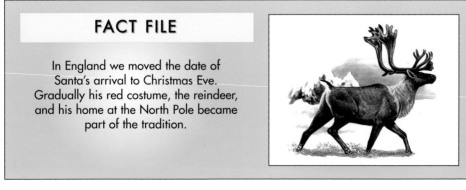

WHO INVENTED THE BICYCLE?

Penny-farthing

FACT FILE

Over the years bicycles have been adapted in many different ways. These wheelchairs are specially built for various sports, including track and field events.

The first designs for people-propelled two-wheeled vehicles date from about 1790. German Karl von Drais made an improved model, the *draisienne*, in about 1817. It had a handlebar to steer the front wheel, but no pedals.

Kirkpatrick Macmillan, a Scottish blacksmith, added pedals to the front wheel in 1839, creating the bicycle, although it had no chain and no gears.

In the 1870s, new designs were made, including the penny-farthing. In 1872, Englishman J. Starley added a chain drive linking the front and rear wheels and in 1885 he produced the first commercial safety bicycle. The invention of pneumatic tyres in 1888 made the machines more comfortable and the most famous cycle race, the Tour de France, was inaugurated a few years later in 1903.

Modern bicycle

WHEN DID SKIING BEGIN?

Skiing is one of the oldest methods of human transport, and may date back as far as 3000 BC, according to archaeologists who have found ancient stone carvings in Sweden and Norway that show people on skis. Early examples of skis have been found in bogs in both Finland and Sweden.

Today, we think of skiing mainly as a winter holiday activity or sporting event, but originally it was used as a way of travelling great distances over snowy ground when walking would have been difficult and too slow, for example, when hunting deer. Skiing remained important throughout Scandinavian history: among the Viking gods were Ull and Skade, the god and goddess of skiing.

FACT FILE

Skiing is a multi-million pound industry for countries such as Italy, the United States of America, France, Switzerland, Austria and Germany.

WHAT IS MRI?

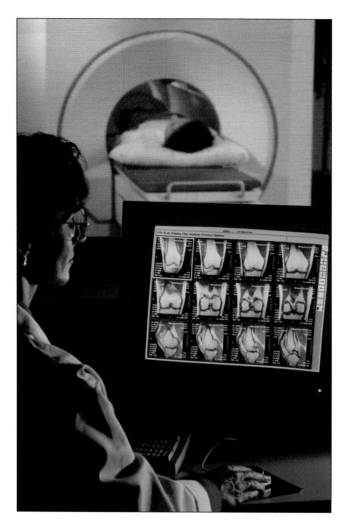

Magnetic resonance imaging (or MRI) is a technique used in medicine for producing images of tissues inside the body. Physicians use these images to diagnose certain diseases, disorders and injuries. MRI is an important diagnostic tool because it enables doctors to identify abnormal tissue without having to open the body through surgery. MRI does not expose the patient to radiation, unlike tests that use x-rays. MRI uses a very powerful magnet and therefore cannot be used on people with metal implants, such as pacemakers, or artificial joints.

FACT FILE

An exciting area of medicine is the Human Genome Project. Its aim is to identify all the 100,000 genes in the human body by studying DNA. This project involves the co-operation of eighteen different countries.

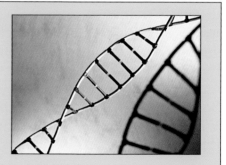

WHICH IS THE WORLD'S LONGEST ROAD SYSTEM?

FACT FILE

Traffic congestion on streets and highways increases travelling times and can also make driving more dangerous. Scientists and engineers are developing intelligent systems to deal with congestion.

The world's longest road system is the Pan American Highway, which criss-crosses Central and South America from the north of Mexico to the south of Chile and links 17 capital cities. The total system covers 29,525 miles (47,516 km). It links up with roads in the United States of America and on to Canada, although these are not officially counted as part of the system.

The main aim of the network is to make the transport of goods easier, both between the countries linked by the network and to the coasts for export elswhere in the world, e.g. coffee and soya from Brazil, beef and corn from Argentina and wine from Chile.

HOW IS CHOCOLATE MADE?

Chocolate is made by processing the beans of the cacao tree, originally found in tropical central America, but now also grown in places such as the Ivory Coast in western Africa.

The Aztecs, who lived in Mexico and areas of Guatemala before the Spanish conquests, made a bitter, spicy cold drink from the bean, which they soaked in water to extract the flavour. The Spanish adapted this to a hot, sweet drink, more like the hot chocolate we know today, although they probably made it with water, not milk.

In order to obtain the chocolate flavour, the cacoa beans are first fermented and then roasted whole. The outer husks are then removed and the beans crushed and the fatty, bitter chocolate extracted. These cocoa solids are used to make sweets and foods.

The different forms of chocolate available include dark (plain), milk and white, which undergo slightly different manufacturing processes. Top quality chocolate contains at least 70 per cent cocoa solids.

FACT FILE

The carob tree has brown, leathery pods that produce a gum. The gum, also called *carob*, has a taste similar to chocolate. After being roasted and ground, it can be substituted for chocolate.

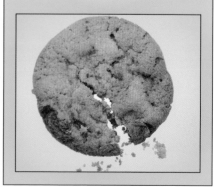

WHAT IS A CALORIE?

230 calories per slice

306 calories

A calorie is a measurement of energy or heat. One calorie is the amount of heat it takes to raise the temperature of one gram of water one degree centigrade. But what does this have to do with food? Well, we eat food to supply us with energy, and so energy in foods is measured in calories. When foods are metabolized – that is, utilized – by being combined with oxygen in the body cells, they give off calories (or energy). In measuring the energy value of food, we use the 'large' or kilogram calorie, which equals one thousand regular calories. Each type of food, as it 'burns up', furnishes a certain number of calories. For instance, one gram of protein provides four calories, but one gram of fat provides nine calories. The amount of calories the body needs depends on the work it has to do.

190 calories

FACT FILE

The body uses up what food it needs and stores some of it for future use. The body can store about one-third of the amount it needs each day. The rest becomes fat!

WHY DOES CORN HAVE SILK?

Whole corn cobs, still in their husks, contain large numbers of long threads that are attached to the main part of the cob. These threads are called corn silk, but they are nothing to do with the silk that is used to produce material.

All plants that produce seed need both male and female parts and corn has both on the same plant (some, like holly and courgettes, have male flowers on some plants and female on others). The male flower on the corn plant is the tassle at the top of the woody stem. The female flowers develop on one or more spikes that grow up the side of the stem. The spikes have rows of female cells, called germ cells or ovules, with a silky thread attached to each. When the male flowers in the field of corn release their pollen, it is caught on the tips of the threads, which stick out from the surrounding husks, and the ovules are fertilized and develop into the seeds, which are called kernels.

FACT FILE

There are five types of corn but popcorn is the only one that pops. The kernels vary greatly in appearance – they may be red, black, gold, off-white or many other colours.

CAN FISH SEE IN THE DARK?

FACT FILE

Like deep-sea shrimp, numerous deepwater fish are bio-luminescent. The anglerfish has a light-producing organ above its mouth to lure prey. The organ is located on a long, flexible spine that looks like a fishing pole.

Fish cannot see in total darkness, but their other senses help them to find food. Some, such as the angler fish, actually carry their own lights.

Oceans offer various habitats at different depths below the surface. These are called zones. The *euphotic* zone is at the top, extending to a depth of about 200 metres (660 ft). Very little light from the Sun can reach further down than this. The *bathypelagic* zone below is totally dark, so no plants can live there, but a number of fish, squid and crustaceans make this zone their home. They feed on waste material that sinks from above.

DO PORCUPINES SHOOT THEIR QUILLS?

Porcupines are plant-eating rodents. They are divided into two groups: Old World, which live in places like Africa and India, have black-and-white striped quills and are ground-dwelling; and New World, which live in forests in North America, have yellowish hair and quills and can climb trees.

The quills are part of the way that porcupines defend themselves even against such large animals as leopards. First, they are raised in a threatening display to make the porcupine look larger: this is usually accompanied by aggressive grunting noises. If cornered, the porcupine will turn and run back at a predator in order to stick its quills in, but no porcupine actually shoots its quills. Many porcupines have barbed quills and if these stick into the predator's flesh, they are impossible to remove and may become infected

FACT FILE

North American porcupines are often incorrectly called hedgehogs. The *common hedgehog* lives in northern Europe, Asia, southern and eastern Africa and New Zealand.

WHAT IS A WASP'S NEST MADE OF?

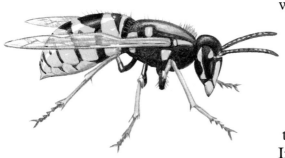

There are two broad groups of wasps, social and solitary. The familiar yellow-and-black stripy wasps belong to the former group and live in colonies that may reach populations of 60,000 by the end of the summer. In the spring, a queen wasp, on waking from winter hibernation, will start a new nest. Some species build nests in trees, while others prefer in a small animal burrow in the ground. She will build a few cells, lay a few eggs to provide herself with workers and put paralysed insects into the cells for the grubs to feed on as they grow. Once hatched, they will take over the work of building cells and finding food.

The cells are made of a form of paper: the wasps chew wood and mix it with saliva to make hexagonal cells. Unlike cells in honeycomb, cells in wasps' nests are arranged in rings and point down.

Solitary wasps lay a few eggs in cells in a hole in the ground and provide food. Solitary wasps have no workers.

FACT FILE

Wasps defend their nests vigorously during the summer months and these should never be approached too closely. All the wasps will die in the winter except the queen, who will go into hibernation.

HOW ARE FIREWORKS MADE?

Firework displays are used to celebrate events all over the world: New Year, Chinese New Year, Diwali – the Hindu Festival of Lights – and, in Britain, Bonfire Night.

Most fireworks consist of a paper tube, containing gunpowder and other chemicals, and a fuse.

Gunpowder – a mixture of potassium nitrate, charcoal and sulphur – was invented in the 11th century (or possibly earlier) in China and was used for fireworks as well as for weapons. In fireworks such as rockets, coarse gunpowder at the base is used to propel the firework into the sky then finer gunpowder, mixed with chemicals that make colour, smoke and loud bangs, explodes. In static fireworks, such as Roman candles, no coarse propellant is used.

FACT FILE

Other chemicals are used to create spectacular fireworks. Powdered titanium burns very rapidly, and results in an almighty boom.

HOW IS SOUND PUT ON A CD?

Compact discs (CDs), CD-Roms, Digital video discs (DVDs) and Minidiscs are all made of a thin layer of metal, usually aluminium, covered in a protective coating of clear, hard plastic. In the case of CDs, sound is translated into electronic signals that are translated into a digital format. This is impressed into the metal of the disc as a series of millions of tiny pits. During playback, a laser reads the changes in the metal and translates these back into sound.

CD-Roms can hold data, and sound files and pictures; DVDs have rapidly overtaken video casettes as a way of playing back movies; and the small size and large memory of minidiscs made them popular.

In the same way that the advent of the CD ousted vinyl singles and albums, improved technology that has led to increased storage capacity on hand-held players, downloading music files from sites on the internet straight to these devices, as well as illegal file-sharing, have led to dramatic reductions in the number of CDs sold.

FACT FILE

Frequency modulation, usually simply called FM, is a method of sending sound signals on radio waves. Amplitude modulation (AM) and FM are the two chief means of transmitting music and speech, although digital technology is increasing in popularity.

WHO DESIGNED SYDNEY OPERA HOUSE?

A Danish designer, Jorn Utzon, won the competition to design Sydney's prestigious new opera house in 1957. His winning plan was chosen from a list of more than 230 entries. Work was started in 1959, but Utzon left in 1966 after delays, political interference over the interior design and disputes about construction. The work was finished, with altered interior designs in 1973. The original cost was meant to be $AU 7,000,000 (£2,800,000), but by completion had spiralled to $AU 10,000,000 (£41,000,000).

Utzon never returned to see his iconic design, but more than 40 years after he left he and his son worked on the refurbishment of the reception in the original style, and it was renamed the Utzon Room in his honour.

FACT FILE

Operas are usually held in special buildings designed to help the whole audience hear the sound clearly. The Opera de la Bastille is the famous opera house in Paris.

WHO WROTE THE FIRST MUSIC?

People in all primitive cultures are thought to have made music. Archaeologists have found such musical instruments as flutes and whistles made of animal bones, as well as cave paintings showing musical instruments being played to accompany dancing. It is thought that singing, music and dance played an important part in religious festivals and ceremonies in many cultures.

For many thousands of years musical, like poetry and stories, would have been an 'oral tradition', that is, one musician would have learned by watching another play and copying. When the ancient Greeks started to write down plays that had singing parts, they needed to indicate the notes and they devised a system that used letters of the alphabet written above the words. Over the centuries, this developed into modern musical notation.

reble clef
hows the
itch

key signature shows
whether the notes should
be flattened or sharpened

FACT FILE

Musical notation is a way of writing down musical sounds so that a singer or instrumentalist can reproduce them as the composer intends.

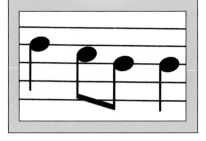

WHEN WAS THE FIRST MAP DRAWN?

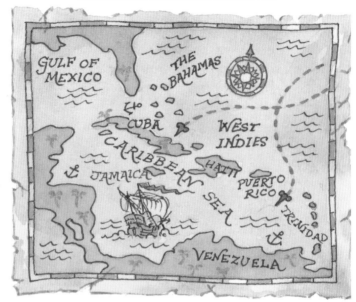

People probably made rough maps even before they began to use written language some 5,500 years ago. A map is an image that represents an area in a way that helps people find places or understand the area's features. Many maps show places or conditions on Earth. Maps may also depict other planets, the Moon, or the position of stars in space. Over the centuries, maps became more accurate as people explored the world and developed better ways to make maps. During the 20th century, people began to use aircraft and spacecraft to observe the Earth and other heavenly bodies. These observations enabled people to create more accurate maps than ever before. In the late 20th century, cartographers made most maps using computers.

FACT FILE

Sailors use nautical charts to help them steer their ships. These charts show water depths, lighthouses, buoys, islands and such dangers as coral reefs and underwater mountains.

WHAT IS A GOBLIN?

The term goblin simply refers to the uglier members of the mythical fairy race. Fairies are small supernatural creatures of human form. They live in our world and are generally thought to be well disposed to humans. However, they have been known to play pranks and it is best to treat them with respect. They are small, beautiful, airy, nearly transparent in body, and can assume any shape. In Ireland, fairies are called *Sidhi*, (pronounced 'shee'). Goblins are particularly unkind to humans, causing mischief, breaking things, switching human babies with changlings, causing insects to plague men and animals, and other such activities. Goblins are said to be most active at Halloween.

FACT FILE

Sometimes there were human-sized fairies, and they were hard to tell from mortals. In Germany, if you met a man with green teeth he was a nix, or a water spirit. When nixes ventured on land, some part of their clothing was always wet.

WHAT IS CURARE?

Curare is a substance obtained from the resin of some plants from tropical South America, chiefly species of *Chondodendron* and *Strychnos.* It is a poisonous member of a group of chemicals called alkaloids. Hunters from some tribes of native South Americans have used it for hundreds of years to tip their arrows.

It disrupts signals from the motor nerves to voluntary and involuntary muscles, so the victim becomes paralyzed and then eventually is unable to breathe.

In small doses, it is used in some operations on the stomach that need the digestive process to be stopped completely and can be used to relax the throat muscles to make some medical examinations easier.

Using poison-tipped arrows is a useful means of ensuring that prey does not escape in dense jungles. Other South American tribes learned to use the poison from the back of certain frogs (known as poison-arrow frogs). The poison from the back of one frog is enough to kill 40 people.

FACT FILE

Many Indians built a pole framework and covered it with leaves or bark, like the dome-shaped wigwam of the Northeast. The Iroquois followed a similar method in building their large, rectangular long houses. Some of these houses were more than 30 m (100 feet) long. The Apache and Paiute used brush and matting to make simple *wickiups*.

HOW OLD ARE THE OLDEST FOSSILS?

Fossils are the impressions in stone of plants and animals that lived long ago. If, for example, a trilobite (left) died and was buried rapidly in sediment its soft body tissue would decay only very slowly and be replaced by minerals from the sediment. Over millions of years, the sediment is compressed into rock and the fossile becomes hard. Among the earliest known fossils are of colonies of bacteria called stromatolites that are more than 3,500 million years old. These bacteria were among the first living organisms on Earth.

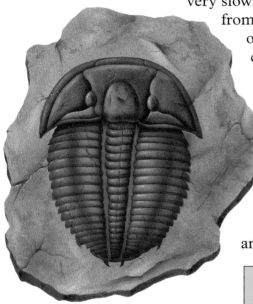

Trilobites and other marine animals appear from about 545 million years ago, while fossils of fish and amphibians are found from about 408 million years ago.

WHEN DID MAN FIRST USE TOOLS?

A tool is any implement that helps us
to do something more easily or more efficiently,
and people have used tools for millions of years. Artefacts
that are recognizably tools consisting of bits of broken stone have
been dated to at least 2,500,000 years ago but sticks and animal
bones and antlers were used long before then.

Palaeontologists define the development of human technology
from the materials that our ancestors used to make tools: the
Palaeolithic (Old Stone Age), when hunter-gatherers used chipped
stone to make hand-axes and scrapers; the Mesolithic (Middle
Stone Age), when tools got more sophisticted; and the Neolithic
(New Stone Age), when people started farming and used polished
stone tools and weapons. The Bronze Age began in about 3,200 BC
in the Middle East and was followed by the Iron Age in about
1,100 BC. Technology took time to travel: the Bronze Age did not
reach Britain until about 2,000 BC.

FACT FILE

Palaeolithic (Old Stone Age)
tools like the axe and scraper
were made from flint. The spear
heads were shaped from deer
antlers. The hand axe was
probably the most important
early Palaeolothic tool.

WHY DO SPIDERS DEPEND ON SILK?

All spiders spin silk, but they do not all use it to create webs. The silk is created in the spiders' silk glands and extruded through little organs at the tip of the abdomen called spinnerets. They either pull the silk out with their back legs or attach it to a fixed object and walk away.

In order to trap prey in their webs, many spiders coat some of the threads (or just one side of them) with a sticky glue and then walk only on the unglued threads to avoid getting stuck themselves. They also have a coating on their feet to help stop them getting caught. Some spiders sit on a patch of dry threads in the centre of the web, whereas others hide at the edge.

Trap-door spiders use their silk to create the hinges of the doors to their lairs, while web-casting spiders make small webs that they hold and then launch at their prey, pinning it to the ground.

Many spiders also use silk to protect their eggs, weaving a small ball of silk around them and anchoring it to something solid.

WHY DO ONIONS MAKE YOU CRY?

When you slice through an onion, you break open a number of onion cells. Some of these cells have enzymes inside them, and when they are sliced open, these enzymes escape. Amino acid is one of the substances that escapes, and it forms itself into a volatile gas. This gas reaches your eyes and reacts with the water that keeps them moist. This changes the chemical's form again, producing, among other things, a mild sulphuric acid, which irritates the eyes. The nerve endings in your eyes are very sensitive and so they pick up on this irritation. This is the reason why our eyes sting when we slice onions. The brain reacts by telling your tear ducts to produce more water, to dilute the irritating acid so the eyes are protected. Your first reaction is probably to rub your eyes, but this will actually make the irritation a lot worse, of course, if you have onion juice all over your hands.

FACT FILE

Not all vegetables grown were always used for food. The ancient Greeks and Romans grew carrots that had thin, tough roots. They used the plants as a medicine but not as a food. Carrots contain *carotene*, a substance used by the human body to produce vitamin A.

HOW DID THE SUNFLOWER GET ITS NAME?

The sunflower got its name because the head of the flower turns and faces towards the Sun throughout the day. The sunflower is a tall plant known for its showy yellow flowers. There are more than 60 species of sunflowers. The most common type grows from 1 to 3 metres (3 to 10 ft) high and has one or more heads of flowers. Each head consists of a disc of small, tubular flowers surrounded by a fringe of large yellow petals. A sunflower head may measure more than 30 cm (1 ft) in diameter and produce up to 1,000 seeds. Sunflower seeds make a very healthy and nutritious snack.

FACT FILE

Sunflower seeds are rich in protein. They yield a high-quality vegetable oil used in making margarine and cooking oil. Some varieties of sunflowers have large, striped seeds, which are roasted for snack food or blended with other grains to make birdseed.

WHAT IS THE EVENING STAR?

FACT FILE

The word planet comes from the Greek for 'wanderer'. Mercury, Venus, Mars, Jupiter, Saturn and Neptune are named after Roman gods, while Uranus and Pluto are Greek gods' names.

The evening star is not, in fact, a star at all, but the planet Venus, which can sometimes be seen close to the western horizon shortly after sunset. When it is on the other side of the Sun it can be seen a while before sunrise above the eastern horizon, when it is known as the morning star. Like all the planets, Venus does not shine, but reflects the light of the Sun. Mercury is also sometimes called an evening or morning star. They can be seen from Earth only when at their farthest east or west of the Sun. When they are closer in they are too faint to be seen.

WHY WAS THE TAJ MAHAL BUILT?

Shah Jahan built the Taj Mahal as a mausoleum for his favourite wife, Arjumand Banu Begum, better known as Mumtaz Mahal ('Elect of the Palace'), who died shortly after giving birth to her fourteenth child, in 1631. Shah Jahan (1592 to 1666) was the fifth ruler of the Mughal empire in India. During his reign, which began in 1628, the Mughals reached their artistic peak, with vast treasures and magnificent architecture. Shah Jahan also built a palace of great beauty in Delhi. These and other buildings still stand as examples of Mughal achievement. The Mughal dynasty began its decline because too much money was spent on luxuries and too much effort was wasted in war. Shah Jahan's reign was a troubled one, and one of his sons eventually took his throne by force.

FACT FILE

Tutankhamun's is the only tomb of an ancient Egyptian king to be discovered almost completely undamaged. Among the items discovered were luxurious chests, thrones, beds, linens, clothing, necklaces, bracelets, rings and earrings.

WHY IS AYERS ROCK SO RED?

Ayers Rock, in Central Australia, consists of arkose, a coarse-grained sandstone which is rich in the mineral feldspar. It is this mineral that gives it its famous red tinge. The flaky surface is caused by the chemical decay of minerals and mechanical erosion. The characteristic rusty appearance of the exposed surface of these flakes is just that – rust. Ayers Rock is believed to have had its beginnings in the Precambrian era about 550 million years ago. Enormous mountain ranges were pushed up then eroded away over the next 200 million years, leaving the Mann, Musgrave and Petermann Ranges in Central Australia. The sediments from these ranges was laid down on the Amadeus Basin, and further earth movements about 300 million years ago began to create the spectacular features we see today.

FACT FILE

The Aboriginal name for Ayers Rock is Uluru – meaning 'great pebble'. Aborigines decorated caves in the rock with paintings.

HOW DOES A PIGEON FIND ITS WAY HOME?

Homing pigeons are well known for their ability to find their way back to their roost, and racing pigeons can fly as much as 800 km (500 miles) in a day to do so. No one is entirely sure how they do this: some scientists think they have an organ within their brains that reads changes in the Earth's magnetic field. When they are close to their home, they also appear to navigate by following landmarks that they have learned to recognize such as roads and rivers.

Some birds that migrate long distances, such as swifts and common terns seem to be born knowing where to fly as the young have to make their own way, while migrating geese, swans and starlings travel in family groups so that the adults can lead the young in the correct direction.

FACT FILE

Homing pigeons have been used to carry messages for more than 3,000 years, including during both World War I and II. The Dickin Medal – known as the animal VC – was awarded to 32 pigeons that flew information across the English channel during World War II.

THE PLANT

WORLD

CONTENTS

· ·

HOW DID FRUITS GET THEIR NAMES?

The names of many fruits are derived from foreign languages, both ancient and modern. Sometimes it is quite surprising to learn how certain names began. Take a word like gooseberry, for example. It has nothing to do with geese. It was originally gorseberry. In Saxon, *gorst* meant rough, and this berry got its name because it grows on a rough or thorny shrub. Raspberry comes from the German verb *raspen*, which means to rub together or rub as with a file. The marks on this berry were thought to resemble a file. Strawberry is a corruption of 'strayberry', and was so named because of the way runners from this plant stray in all directions. The cranberry was once called the 'craneberry', because the slender stalks resemble the long legs and neck of the crane. The term grape is the English equivalent of the Italian *grappo*, and the Dutch and French *grappe*, all of which mean a 'bunch'. Melon is the Greek word for apple, while tomato is the West Indian name for love-apple.

FACT FILE

Botanists classify tomatoes as fruits. Horticulturists, however, classify them as vegetables. Most other people consider tomatoes to be vegetables because they are used in much the same way as many other vegetables.

WHAT IS POISON IVY?

Poison ivy is a kind of harmful vine or shrub belonging to the cashew family. It grows plentifully in parts of the United States and southern Canada. Poison ivy usually grows as a vine, twining on tree trunks or straggling over the ground. The plant often forms bushes if it has no support to climb on. The tissues of these plants contain a poisonous oil somewhat like carbolic acid. This oil is extremely irritating to the skin and it can be brushed onto the clothing or skins of people coming in contact with the plants. The leaves of poison ivy are red in early spring. Later they change to shiny green, while in autumn they turn red or orange. Each leaf is made up of three leaflets more or less notched at the edges. Later in the season, clusters of poisonous, berrylike drupes form. They are whitish, with a waxy look.

FACT FILE

Ground ivy is a trailing, fragrant plant that has creeping stems which form thick masses of leaves wherever they get a hold. Ground ivy was formerly used in making ale and cough medicine.

WHAT ARE SUCCULENTS?

Cacti

FACT FILE

Cacti have many rare and beautiful features, developed during a long and slow evolutionary process. One of their principal characteristics is the ability to adapt to harsh conditions which would cause most other plant groups to perish quickly.

Succulents are plants that have leaves, stems or roots that can store water so that they can survive extended periods of drought. All the plants in the cactus family are considered stem succulents. During periods of moisture, their stems swell and then during droughts they slowly contract. Cacti with ribs are particularly well adapted to surviving droughts as their ribs expand and contract like an accordion. Cacti get their name from the Greek word *kaktos* meaning thistle.

WHAT IS DODDER?

Dodder is a strange, totally parasitic plant. When its tiny seeds start to grow, they put up thin threads that twist in ever-increasing circles. Most seedlings die, because they fail to find the right sort of plant to take their food from. But if one seed finds the right host, it quickly attaches itself and pushes absorbing organs into the plant. The root of the seed then withers and dies, since the dodder plant now takes all of its food from its host. The most popular host plants are alfalfa, clover and flax. Dodder has tiny pink leaves that have no need for chlorophyll, which enables most plants to make food from sunlight. In late summer, dodder produces small, pink flowers, and then masses of tiny seeds.

FACT FILE

Once dodder has established itself, it produces a mass of pink threads which cover the host plant and weaken it severely.

CAN PLANTS FEEL?

FACT FILE

Some plants have sensitive hairs on their leaves. If an unsuspecting insect lands on these sticky hairs, it will quickly find its legs hopelessly entangled.

Although plants do not have feelings in the same way that we do, they can certainly respond to different stimuli. They are able to grow towards a light source, even if turned upside down. Some plants have very sensitive leaves, which will fold up if touched. Others have leaves that open and close according to the time of day. The Venus Flytrap has sensitive leaf tips. When an insect lands on the tiny hairs on the leaf, the pairs of leaves snap shut, trapping the insect inside. Plants are even able to perspire. Although you can't see this happening, if you were to place a plant inside a plastic bag and fasten it, after a while you would see drops of water form on the inside of the bag. The moisture you can see comes from the leaves of the plant.

Lords and ladies

WHICH PLANT APPEARS TO FLOAT ON WATER?

The water lily, also called the pond lily, is a large, aquatic plant which appears to float on water. Water lilies send their long, strong leaves and flower stalks up from the muddy bottom below clear, shallow water. Their kidney-shaped, green leaves are usually seen floating on the surface of the water but may also be submerged. The flowers are usually raised above the water on long stalks. The white-flowered water lily is the most common. The flowers may be as large as 30 cm (1 foot) across. Their fruits, when ripe, look like old-fashioned brandy bottles. Some water lilies bloom during the day and others during the night.

FACT FILE

Yellow water lilies are found in lakes, ponds and rivers. Bulrushes grow in marshes or in shallow water. They have tough stems which are round or triangular and up to 3.7 m (12 feet) tall. Their tiny flowers are clustered into small brownish spikelets at or near the tops of the stems.

113

WHAT IS THE OTHER NAME FOR THE IRIS?

Yellow flag iris

Fleur-de-lis is a name sometimes used for the iris. It is French for flower of the lily. Fleur-de-lis is also the name of a design that represents the white iris. It appeared as an emblem on the sceptre of Egyptian rulers in 1500 BCE, and was carved on the brow of the Sphinx. It also became the emblem of the kings of France in the 12th century.

The name 'iris' comes from the Greek word for *rainbow*. The unusual shape of the iris makes it easy to recognize. An iris has three sets of three petal-like parts. The lower set, called the falls, flares out and hangs down. The upper parts, known as standards, curve up into a dome. Three curved style branches cover the stamens in the middle.

FACT FILE

King Charles V of France adopted three golden fleurs-de-lis on a blue field as his coat of arms in the 14th century. The design is also a symbol for north on the compass.

WHY IS HOLLY ASSOCIATED WITH CHRISTMAS?

Holly has been used traditionally in houses and churches at Christmastime for decorative purposes. It was originally called the *holy tree*. The word holly may have come from this name. Holly is the common name for a group of shrubs and small trees. The two best-known hollies, the American holly and the English holly, are evergreens. These two hollies have glossy green leaves and red berries and are used to make attractive Christmas wreaths. Holly wood is very hard and has a close grain. It is used for making musical instruments, furniture and in interior decoration. The inner bark yields the sticky material called birdlime. The leaves of a South American species are used to make a tea-like drink called mate.

FACT FILE

The poinsettia is a popular houseplant also used as a Christmas decoration. What look like the bright red petals are actually a kind of leaf. The real flowers are the tiny green dots in the middle.

IS THERE REALLY A FOUR-LEAVED CLOVER?

A particular feature of the clovers is their three-lobed (or trifoliate) leaves. The lucky 'four-leaved clover' can be found, but it is an abnormal rarity. Clovers are members of the pea family. There are around 250 kinds of true clovers, including the red, white, strawberry and crimson species. Clovers are generally grassland plants and they are most common near the coast and on chalky or clay soils. Red clover has been used for centuries as a rotation crop. Today, it is used extensively as an animal food and soil-improving crop throughout Europe and northern and central North America.

FACT FILE

Clover flowers are very rich in nectar and so attract many insects. The white base of the flower has a lovely taste like fresh honey.

DOES BINDWEED ALWAYS TWINE IN THE SAME DIRECTION?

It is a curious fact that all bindweed plants twine around their supporting plant in the same direction – anticlockwise – which ever way they start off. The Greater Bindweed, or Hedge Convolvulus, is a hedge plant found abundantly throughout England and Scotland. Despite the beauty of its flowers, bindweed is regarded as a pest by both the farmer and the gardener. Its roots are long and form a dense mass that exhausts the soil. Its twining stems extend in masses over all other nearby plants, consequently strangling them.

FACT FILE

If a gardener were to turn it in another direction and the bindweed could not untangle itself and assume its natural direction from right to left, it would eventually die.

WHAT ARE GRAPES USED FOR?

A grape is a juicy, smooth-skinned berry that grows on a woody vine. Grapes grow in clusters of as few as six to as many as 300 berries. The berries may be black, blue, golden, green, purple, red or white, depending on the variety of the plant. About 60 million metric tonnes (66 million short tons) of grapes are harvested annually throughout the world. About 80 per cent are used in making wine and about 13 per cent are sold as fresh grapes. The rest is used for drying into raisins, for making juice or jelly, and in canning with other fruits. Grapes have a high sugar content, which makes them a good source of energy.

FACT FILE

Most wine grapes are picked by machine. However, special grapes for making rare wines are carefully picked by hand.

WHO INTRODUCED THE DANDELION?

FACT FILE

When the flowers of the dandelion mature, they form feathered, cottony seeds that the wind carries far and wide.

The early colonists brought the dandelion to America from Europe. Its name comes from the French words *dent de lion*, meaning lion's tooth.

The dandelion is a bright yellow wild flower that grows in lawns and meadows. Throughout the temperate regions of the world, gardeners usually consider the dandelion a troublesome weed that is difficult to control. It has smooth leaves with coarse notches, which look like teeth. The golden yellow head is really a cluster of flowers. The dandelion has a smooth, straight, hollow stem, and the entire plant contains a white, milky juice. The root is long, thick and pointed and has hairlike branches growing from it.

The dandelion differs from most other plants in the way it reproduces. Its ovaries form fertile seeds without having to be pollinated.

WHAT ARE CHANTERELLES?

Chanterelles are mushroom-like fungi with funnel-shaped caps. The delicious and fragrant golden chanterelle is a delicacy prized by gourmets. Chanterelles are characterized by the form of their spore-producing surface, which is smooth and veined.

Mushrooms are important to our environment as they help keep soil fertile for the growth of other plants. As mushrooms grow, they cause the decay of the materials from which they obtain food. This process releases important minerals into the soil. Plants use these minerals to grow and stay healthy.

Mushrooms are also an important source of food for insects and many small animals. Red squirrels collect mushrooms in the summer and let them dry on tree branches, then they store them for use as a winter food.

Golden chanterelle

Trumpet chanterelle

FACT FILE

The term tooth-fungi covers a range of unrelated species all of which have spines or teeth on which spores are produced. Because of pollution, many of these are becoming rare.

WHICH IS THE
LARGEST KNOWN FUNGI?

The giant puffball is the largest known fungi. It can grow as large as 150 cm (60 inches), although an average fruitbody is the size of a football. Just one fruitbody will produce about 7,000,000,000,000 spores. The puffballs are ball-shaped fungi, and may be any shade from white to tan. They range in size from smaller than a golfball to larger than a basketball. When a puffball matures, its spores become dry and powdery. If touched, the puffball breaks open and the spores escape in a smokelike puff.

Black bovista

Scaly meadow puffball

FACT FILE

Flies and other insects are attracted to the stinking, slimy spore mass of the common stinkhorn. When they fly off after feeding, they carry away spores stuck on to their bodies. This is the way in which the stinkhorn spreads to new locations.

WHICH PLANT IS USED TO THATCH A ROOF?

Reed is a common name for many kinds of tall, slender grass plants which are used to thatch houses. The word may also refer to the stems of these plants, which are often jointed in many places. The stems can be as slender and fragile as straw, or as thick and sturdy as bamboo. The pith that fills the centre of the reed can usually be removed, leaving a hollow, jointed tube.

Common reeds are cut and used to make thatched roofs, which is a skilled craft. The thatch provides good heat insulation for the house.

Reeds grow in almost all countries in the temperate and warm regions. They are found in a variety of habitats, from low upland meadows to wet lowlands and shallow lakes and ponds.

Common reed

FACT FILE

In many wetland areas, reeds spread rapidly, crowding out other types of marsh grass. For this reason it has to be regularly cut down. Reed grass has been used in the production of paper.

WHAT IS THE FRUIT OF THE OAK?

The acorn is the fruit of the oak tree. In the spring, oaks produce small, yellowish-green flowers. The male flowers, which form in dangling clusters called catkins, produce large amounts of pollen. The wind carries the pollen to the female flowers and fertilizes them. Once fertilized, a female flower will become an acorn. Acorns vary in length from less than 13 mm ($^1/_2$ inch) to more than 5 cm (2 inches).

Oaks grow slowly and usually do not bear acorns until they are about 20 years old. Most oaks live for 200 to 400 years.

FACT FILE

The Oak Leaf Roller Moth lays small groups of eggs on oak twigs. In spring, the caterpillar feeds on oak leaves, which they roll up with silk.

WHY DO PLANTS NEED ROOTS?

Roots are not pretty and bright like leaves and flowers, but most plants could not survive without them. Anchored in the soil, they hold plants upright against wind and weather. They also grow out and down in search of water and minerals which are drawn all the way up to the leaves. Because trees

grow to such enormous heights, their roots need to grow outwards to balance the spread of the branches above. Most

FACT FILE

There is one plant that survives without any roots at all, and that is Spanish moss. This grows in subtropical climates where the air is very wet. It absorbs all the moisture it needs through its fine, thread-like leaves.

roots grow in the top 30 cm (12 inches) of soil. This part contains most of the important minerals the tree needs to survive. Every single root grows a mass of tiny hairs near its tip to enable it to asborb water from the soil. There are little pockets of air in the soil. Without these, roots would simply wither and die.

WHICH PLANTS HAVE NO TRUE ROOTS?

Liverwort

Liverworts, hornworts and mosses do not have true roots. Instead, they are anchored to the ground by hair-like structures called *rhizoids* that resemble roots. A liverwort absorbs water over its entire surface and dries out quickly. Consequently, liverworts grow extremely close to the ground and often measure less than 1.4 cm (¹/₂ inch) high.

Most liverworts grow only in damp, shady environments, such as rotten logs, stream banks, and moist cliffs.

Moss has a short stem which grows from the rhizoids. It is covered by tiny leaves in a spiral pattern. The leaves contain chlorophyll, a green substance that the plant uses to make food. In many cases, a vein runs the length of the leaf from the stem to the tip. This vein, called the costa or midrib, strengthens the leaf and transports food and water. Many mosses grow in moist or aquatic environments.

However, some mosses can survive in very dry conditions. Their need for water changes with the amount of water available in the environment.

FACT FILE

Lichens have no roots. They have an outer layer of fungal cells that are pigmented green, brown or yellow. This protective layer, called the upper cortex, covers a zone of green or blue-green algal cells.

Moss

HOW DO LEAF SHAPES VARY?

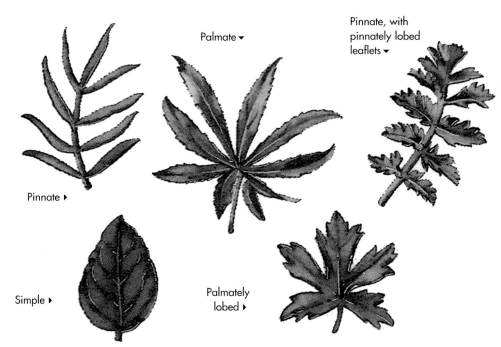

Palmate ▾

Pinnate, with pinnately lobed leaflets ▾

Pinnate ▶

Simple ▶

Palmately lobed ▶

The shapes of plant leaves vary considerably. The edges of leaves may be smooth or jagged. The leaf blades may be undivided (simple), or they may be divided (lobed) in various ways. Some leaves may be made up of separate leaflets. The commonest types of leaf shape are shown above.

The leaves themselves may be arranged on the plant in different ways, and this is usually standard for any given type of plant. A leaf arrangement which has single leaves at each level is called alternate. Leaves arranged in pairs are known as opposite. Opposite leaves may all face the same way, or each pair may be set at right angles to the pair below.

FACT FILE

Some plants have all their leaves in a ring at the base of the stem. This is known as a rosette.

HOW ARE FLOWERS ARRANGED?

FACT FILE

Although flowers vary enormously in appearance, they generally have the same fundamental parts.

Sepal   Stamen   Petal

Style   Ovary

Flowers are produced in many different arrangements on different plants. Solitary flowers are borne singly, with one flower on each stem. Other arrangements are far more complex. A group of flowers together on one plant is called an inflorescence. The patterns of the branching flowers in an inflorescence tend to be the same for a given type of plant. The most common flower arrangements are shown below.

Panicle

Raceme (each flower has a stalk)

Spike

Solitary

Single umbel

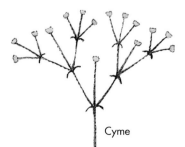

Cyme

WHY DO WE KISS UNDER MISTLETOE?

Early European peoples used mistletoe as a ceremonial plant, and the custom of using mistletoe as a decoration at Christmastime probably comes from this practice. In many places, tradition says that a person caught standing beneath the mistletoe must forfeit a kiss. Mistletoe is an evergreen with oblong, leathery leaves. It has tiny yellow flowers that bloom in February and March. Mistletoe lives by taking some of the nutrients it needs from trees and has no contact with the ground. The trees the mistletoe may grow on include apple, lime, hawthorn, sycamore, poplar, locust, fir and occasionally oak. Mistletoe is associated with many traditions and holidays, especially Christmas. Historians say the Druids cut the mistletoe that grew on the sacred oak and gave it to the people for charms. In Teutonic mythology, an arrow of mistletoe killed Balder, son of the goddess Frigg.

FACT FILE

Birds eat the white, shiny berries of the mistletoe. The berry seeds cling to the birds' bills and are scattered when birds sharpen their bills against the bark of trees.

WHERE DID THE FIRST WILD STRAWBERRY GROW?

FACT FILE

Strawberries grow wild or are raised commercially in almost every country. Plant breeders have developed hundreds of varieties of strawberries that are suited for different growing conditions.

Wild strawberries first grew in ancient Rome. During the 18th century, a hybrid variety was developed in France by breeding wild strawberries brought from North America with others from Chile. The first important American variety, the Hovey, was grown in 1834 in Massachusetts.

The strawberry, a small plant of the rose family, is grown for its tasty heart-shaped fruit. Strawberry plants grow close to the ground and produce small, white flowers with a pleasant smell. The fruit is greenish white at first and ripens to a bright red. It is a good source of vitamin C and is often eaten fresh. Strawberries are also frozen and canned and used in making jam, jelly and wine.

HOW DID THE TIGER LILY GET ITS NAME?

The tiger lily is a tall, hardy garden flower named for its black-spotted, reddish-orange petals, which resemble a tiger's pelt. A few varieties have red, white or yellow petals. The lily first grew in China, Japan and Korea but has become a popular garden plant in North America and Europe.

Tiger lily stems are greenish-purple or dark brown, and many grow from 1.2 to 1.5 metres (4 to 5 feet) high. There may be up to 20 flowers on a stem. The leaves are long and spear-shaped. Tiger lily plants grow from bulbs. Tiny black bulbils (bulblets) develop where the leaves join the stalk. The bulbils eventually drop off, producing new plants. Tiger lilies grow best in bright sunlight and in well-drained, slightly acid soil.

FACT FILE

Magnolia trees are one of the oldest flowering plants. They have been around for one hundred million years, and are still flourishing today.

WHAT ARE THE OLDEST KINDS OF PLANTS ON EARTH?

Ferns are among the oldest kinds of plants that live on land. Scientists believe that ferns appeared on Earth more than 350 million years ago. Ferns differ from flowering plants mainly in the way that they reproduce. They do not have seeds, but reproduce by means of microscopic spores, and they have fronds instead of true leaves. Microscopic spores are produced on the underside of these fronds, and these are scattered by the wind. When the spores land in a suitably damp area, they sprout and grow into a tiny plant that develops small reproductive structures. Sperms fertilize the egg cell, which begins to grow as the tiny plant shrivels and dies, and the complete fern begins to develop.

WHERE DOES THE WORD LAVENDER COME FROM?

Lavender comes from a Latin word that means to wash. This name may have been used because the ancient Romans used the leaves and flowers of the plant to scent their bathwater.

In the past, women used to keep dried lavender flowers with their linen and clothing. Today, the dried flowers are used in fragrant sachets and potpourri mixtures. The flowers are also distilled to make an oil that is used in some perfumes.

Lavender has long, narrow, pale green leaves and pale purple flowers. This shade of purple is called lavender after the flowers. The flowers grow in clusters around the stem. When dried, they keep their fragrance for a long time.

Potpourri

FACT FILE

The petals of certain flowers contain sweet-smelling oils. Such flowers include jasmines, mimosas and roses. The oils obtained from the petals of these flowers supply the fragrances for many high quality perfumes.

HOW DID THE IDEA OF AROMATHERAPY DEVELOP?

Aromatherapy as an art and practice has been traced back about 5000 years, though its origins are probably as old as the discovery of fire. It was the ancient Egyptians who first worked to perfect the practice of aromatherapy. They came to believe that plants that could evoke such results must be gifts of their gods and hence incorporated aromatherapy into their religious ceremonies. These ancient peoples used to perform sacred ceremonies in honour of their gods, burning incense and anointing their bodies with precious oils. Large quantities of aromatics were burned in public places to purify the air and drive away 'evil spirits', which we may think of as emotional distress or similar afflictions.

FACT FILE

In ancient Africa, some of the people discovered that by rubbing certain plants on their skin, greater protection from the Sun was provided by the oils that these plants left behind. In addition, these oils helped to prevent skin afflictions and to maintain softness.

WHAT IS MADE FROM THE WILLOW TREE?

Willow trees usually live in moist habitats such as flood plains and on river banks, where they grow very rapidly. Their wood is used in many ways, and their leaves supply food for wildlife. Twigs of the common osier are grown for use in basketmaking, and the light but dent-resistant wood of other willows is used for artificial limbs, wooden shoes and cricket bats. Willow bark contains the active compound salicin, used in many folk medicines. Aspirin is a derivative of salicylic acid, which was first synthesized from derivatives of willow bark.

FACT FILE

Willow pattern china originated in Staffordshire, England, c.1780. Thomas Minton, then an apprentice potter, developed and engraved the design, taken from an old Chinese legend.

WHAT IS BARK?

Bark is the outer covering of the stem of woody plants, composed of waterproof cork cells. This protects a layer of food-conducting tissue called the *phloem* or inner bark (also called *bast*). As the woody stem increases in size, the outer bark of dead cork cells gives way – it may split to form grooves, shred, as in the cedar, or

peel off, as in the sycamore. A layer of reproductive cells called the *cork cambium* produces new cork cells to replace or reinforce the old ones. Trees are sometimes damaged by animals that eat the outer bark, cutting through the phloem tubes; this can result in starvation of the roots and, ultimately, the death of the tree.

The outer bark of the paper birch was used by Native Americans to make baskets and canoes.

FACT FILE

Bottle corks are made from the thick, spongy bark of the cork oak, which grows in the Mediterranean region. Oaks produce durable, tough wood and are important timber trees.

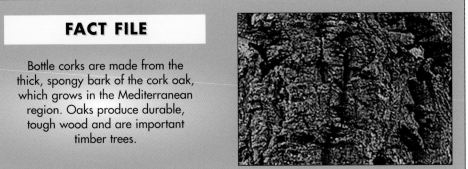

WHAT IS PEAT?

Peat is partly decayed plant matter that has collected in swamps and marshes over long periods of time. It is formed by the slow decay of successive layers of aquatic and semiaquatic plants such as sedges, reeds, rushes and mosses.

Dried peat is used mainly as a fuel in places where coal and oil are scarce. In Ireland, for example, peat is a major source of fuel to generate electricity. Dried peat varies from a light yellow-brown substance resembling tangled hay, to deeper layers of dark brown, compact material that looks like brown coal. Some peat is still dug and stacked by hand.

Black peat is used as a fertilizer. Fluffy brown peat is used as a packing material, and as bedding for farm animals. One of the principal types of peat is moss peat, derived primarily from sphagnum moss; it is used in agriculture as poultry and stable litters as well as mulch, a soil conditioner.

FACT FILE

Peat is the earliest stage of transition from compressed plant growth to the formation of coal. The oldest coal was formed 350 million years ago, and the process still continues in swamps and bogs.

Sphagnum moss

WHY DOES A PINE TREE HAVE CONES?

A pine tree has cones in order to reproduce. The pine cone is actually a highly modified branch which takes the place of a flower. Separate male cones and female seed cones are borne on the same tree. Each of the numerous scales of the male cone bears pollen, while each female cone scale bears ovules in which egg cells are produced. In the pine the male cones are small and short-lived, and are borne in clusters at the top of the tree. At the time of pollination, enormous numbers of pollen grains are released and dispersed by the wind. Those that land accidentally on female cone scales extend pollen tubes part way into the ovule during one growing season but usually do not reach the stage of actual fertilization until the next year. The cones that are usually seen are the seed cones, which are normally hard and woody.

FACT FILE

Scots pine trees need to be tough to survive long, cold winters. They have thousands of tiny, needle-like leaves, which have a waterproof coating to protect them from the rain and snow.

WHAT ARE STOMATA?

Stomata are tiny holes in leaves, which a plant can open and close. When the stomata are open, they let air in and out and water out. When the stomata are closed, water cannot escape from the leaves.

Plants absorb water from the soil through their roots. This water moves up the stem to the leaves, where about 90 per cent evaporates through the stomata. Large trees lose more than 800 litres (200 gallons) of water from their leaves each day. This loss of water from leaves by evaporation is called transpiration. Other plant processes that involve water include photo-synthesis, which uses  water to make food, and respiration, in which water is produced. When it is dark, plants shut down for the night by closing their stomata.

WHICH IS THE BIGGEST FLOWER OF ALL?

FACT FILE

Green algae are the smallest plants. They form a greenish film often found on the bark of trees, for example. Millions of algae cells are needed to cover a tree trunk.

The biggest flower of all is called the *rafflesia*, a parasitic plant that does not photosynthesize. It grows in the rainforests of southeast Asia. The plant actually grows underground and is not visible until a huge bud appears, somewhat like a cabbage. This opens up into a leathery flower which is approximately 1 metre (3 feet) across and weighs up to 10 kg (22 lb). The flower is not a pretty sight, it looks and smells just like a huge lump of rotting flesh. It attracts thousands of flies, which pollinate the flower as they walk on it.

THE

HUMAN BODY

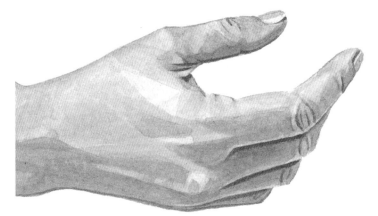

Contents

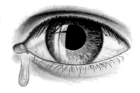

WHEN DO YOU LOSE YOUR BABY TEETH?

The first set of teeth we have is the baby, milk or deciduous set. Even before birth, teeth appear as tiny buds below the gums. They begin to show above the gum from the age of a few months. By the age of about three, all 20 first teeth have usually appeared. From about the age of six, the first teeth fall out. These are replaced by the adult, second or permanent teeth. First are usually the front incisors and the first molars, at around seven to eight years. The last to appear are the rearmost molars, or wisdom teeth. Some adults never grow wisdom teeth. In many cases, the jaws do not grow large enough to provide space for the wisdom teeth. As a result, the wisdom teeth may become impacted – that is, wedged between the jawbone and another tooth. If this happens, the wisdom teeth must be removed.

FACT FILE

Because we eat such a variety of food we have different types of teeth. Each type does a different job:

1. incisors – cut
2. canines – tear
3. premolars
4. molars
} crush and grind

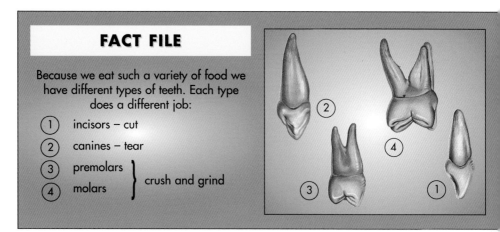

WHAT'S INSIDE A TOOTH?

A tooth consists of four kinds of tissues. They are (1) pulp (2) dentine (3) enamel and (4) cementum.

Pulp is the innermost layer of a tooth. It consists of connective tissue, blood vessels and nerves. The blood vessels nourish the tooth. The nerves transmit sensations of pain to the brain.

Dentine is a hard, yellow substance that surrounds the pulp. It makes up most of a tooth. Dentine is harder than bone. It consists mainly of mineral salts and water but also has some living cells.

Enamel overlays the dentine in the crown of the tooth. It forms the outermost covering of the crown. Enamel is the hardest tissue in the body. It enables a tooth to withstand the pressure placed on it during chewing. Cementum overlays the dentine in the root of the tooth. In most cases, the cementum and enamel meet where the root ends and the crown begins. As the surface of the tooth wears away, the tooth grows farther out of its socket, exposing the root.

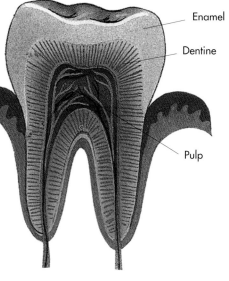

Enamel

Dentine

Pulp

FACT FILE

Sometimes teeth grow crookedly or become overcrowded in the mouth. This can be put right by wearing teeth braces. Braces consist of metal or clear ceramic brackets that are bonded on the front surface of each tooth and connected by wires.

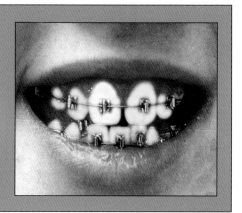

WHAT ARE SYNOVIAL JOINTS?

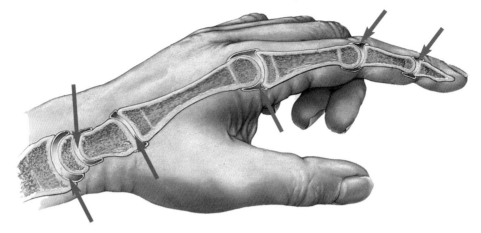

Synovial joints, for example, the elbow, knuckles and wrists are designed to allow a large range of movements and are lined with a slippery coating called synovium. Some joints in the body only allow a small amount of movement between the bones, but if their effect is combined with lots of joints in close proximity, the result is greater flexibility. The bones in the wrist, ankle and spinal column all work like this. In the synovial joint the ends of the bones are held together by tough straps called ligaments. These bridge the gap between the bones and are anchored onto them at each end. Where bone ends move against each other, they are covered with cartilage, or gristle. This is shiny, smooth and slightly rubbery. It allows the bone ends to slide past each other with very little friction.

FACT FILE

The knee is unusual because it has straps of ligaments called cruciate (cross-shaped) ligaments inside the joint, as well as ligaments outside. It also has two crescent-shaped pieces of cartilage called *menisci*, that 'float' between the bone ends.

WHAT DOES A TENDON SHEATH PROTECT?

The tendon sheath is a double-walled sleeve designed to isolate, protect and lubricate the tendon to reduce the possibility of damage from pressure or friction. The space between the two layers of the tendon sheath contains fluid so that these layers slide over each other easily. A tendon, also called a sinew, is a strong white cord that attaches muscles to bones. Muscles move bones by pulling on tendons.

A tendon is a cordlike bundle of connective tissue. Some tendons are round, others are long or flat. One end of a tendon rises from the end of a muscle; the other end is woven into the substance of a bone. The tendon may slide up and down inside a sheath of fibrous tissue, in the same way that an arm moves in a coat sleeve. Tendons at the ankle and wrist are enclosed in sheaths at the points where they cross or are in close contact with other structures.

Tendon sheath

Tendons

FACT FILE

Most muscles can be controlled by consciously thinking about them – they move when you want them to. They are called voluntary muscles and there are more than 600 of them in your body. We use 200 voluntary muscles every time we take a step.

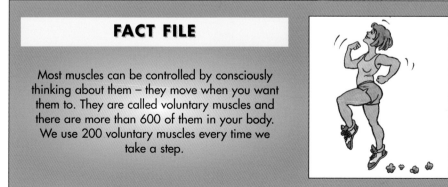

WHAT PURPOSE DO TEARS SERVE?

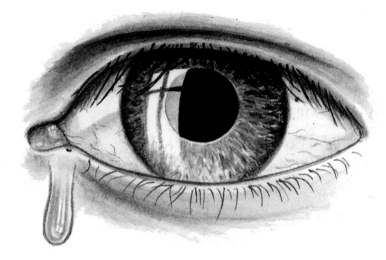

Tears are the secretion of the lacrimal glands. They continually bathe the cornea, the tough outer layer of the eyeball. They help to clear it of foreign particles, such as dust and hairs, and keep it from drying out, which would result in blindness. Two lacrimal glands, one over each eye, lie behind the eyelid. They pour out their fluid through several small ducts in the underside of the eyelid. Each time a person blinks an eyelid, it sucks a little fluid from the glands. When a person feels some emotion very strongly, such as grief or anger, the muscles around the lacrimal glands may tighten up and squeeze out the tear fluid. The same thing happens if a person laughs very heartily. After the tears pass across the eyeball, they flow out through two lacrimal ducts that open at the inner corner of each eye.

FACT FILE

Mostly a salt solution, lacrimal fluid also contains substances that fight bacteria, and proteins that help make the eye immune to infection.

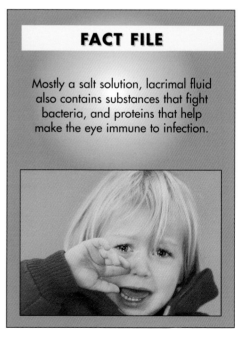

WHY DO OUR PUPILS CHANGE SIZE?

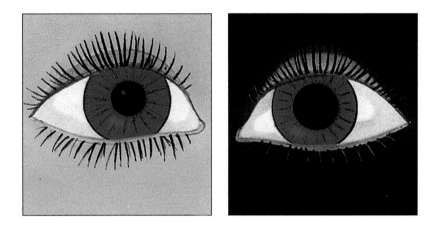

The coloured part of our eyes is called the iris, and the opening in its centre is called the pupil. In bright light conditions, the sphincter muscle in the iris reduces the size of the pupil so that less light enters the eye and in low light levels the dilator muscle expands the pupil to allow as much light into the eye as possible. The pigment that gives the iris colour is called melatonin.

Because humans evolved to be awake during the day and sleep at night we do not need particularly good night vision, while cats, which in the wild are more nocturnal and hunt at night and sleep during the day, can see much better in the dark than we can.

FACT FILE

Birds have the keenest sight of all animals, including human beings. An osprey (right) can see a dead animal on the ground from a height of up to 4 km (2^1/$_2$ miles).

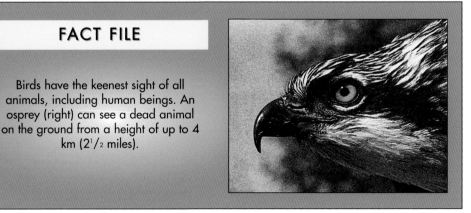

WHAT IS GENETIC ENGINEERING?

Genetic engineering (which is sometimes called genetic modification) is the science of altering the genetic codes deep within our cells. It is hoped that in future genetic engineering can be used to cure genetic disorders such as cystic fibrosis by replacing a faulty gene with a properly functioning one.

The inside of a cell

In agriculture, people have deliberately cross-bred plants and animals to produce desirable traits for thousands of years, and now gene-splicing techniques are being used in the same way, for example, to create crops that are resistant to diseases and pests or need less water than 'natural' varieties, and animals that produce more milk or grow more quickly.

The nucleus is the focu point of the cell, containing the genetic information as strands of DNA.

FACT FILE

Researchers have found important uses for genetic engineering in such fields as medicine, industry and agriculture. Many new uses are predicted for the future.

HOW DOES OUR IMMUNE SYSTEM WORK?

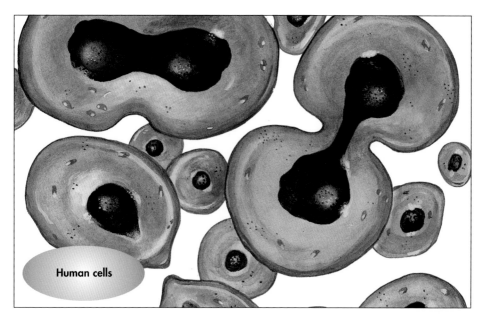

Human cells

The immune system is a group of cells, molecules and tissues that help defend the body against diseases and other harmful invaders. The immune system provides protection against a variety of potentially damaging substances that can invade the body. These substances include disease-causing organisms, such as bacteria, fungi, parasites and viruses. The body's ability to resist these invaders is called immunity.

A key feature of the immune system is its ability to destroy foreign invaders while leaving the body's own healthy tissues untouched. Sometimes, however, the immune system attacks and damages these healthy tissues. This reaction is called an autoimmune response or autoimmunity.

FACT FILE

The immune response is the body's reaction to the invasion of foreign substances by the production of white blood cells known as lymphocytes. Lymphocytes are mainly produced in bone marrow.

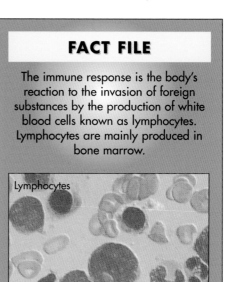

Lymphocytes

HOW DO FINGERPRINTS DIFFER?

Fingerprints have fascinated people for centuries. They have been used as a method of personal identification since ancient times. But where do fingerprints come from and is it true that they are all different? If you look very closely at a fingerprint, you will notice that

it is made up of ridges on the skin. These ridges aren't always continuous; they stop, split into two, form little pockets (called 'lakes') and even appear to cross each other at times. It is these individual features that make the difference between one fingerprint and the next.

Fingerprints are formed before birth, during the development of the hands. Fingerprints are not actually formed in the skin, but are caused by ridges in the flesh underneath the skin. Genetics plays some part in their formation, but even identical twins have different fingerprints. Fingerprints fall into a set number of patterns, which allows us to catalogue them and perform fingerprint searches more easily.

FACT FILE

How do you leave a fingerprint at the scene of a crime? Skin pores produce oils and sweat, which are distributed on your fingers. When you touch something, those liquids are left on the surface, in the shape of your fingerprints

WHAT MAKES HAIR CURLY?

Skin feels smooth, but under a microscope it looks like a jagged mountain range with huge pits sprouting hair. These pits are

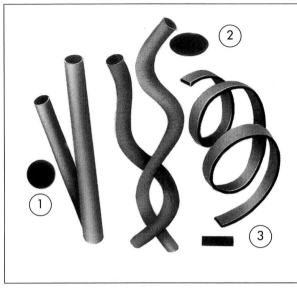

called follicles, and they make hair straight or curly. Straight hair grows from a round follicle (1), wavy hair grows from an oval-shaped one (2), and very curly hair grows from a flat one (3).

The texture of hair depends largely on the shape of the hair, which can be seen in cross-section under a microscope. Straight hairs have a round shape, and wavy and curly hairs are flat. The flattest hairs are the waviest or curliest.

The number of hairs you have on your head depends on whether you are a blonde or brunette. Most blondes have about 140,000 head hairs, redheads average 90,000, while people with black or brown hair come somewhere in the middle with about 110,000 hairs.

Most hair follicles contain an oil gland called the sebaceous gland. This gland secretes oil into the follicle. The oil flows over the hair, lubricating it and keeping it soft.

FACT FILE

Most people's hair gradually becomes grey or white as they grow older, because the pigment (called melanin) which gives hair its colour, no longer forms.

WHAT IS THE OLFACTORY SYSTEM?

The olfactory system is the scientific term for our sense of smell. Your smell receptors are in the upper half of your nose, in a space called the nasal cavity. Smell receptors are affected by scent particles – tiny chemical units called molecules in the air you breathe. Each receptor cell has minute hairs which are covered with sticky mucus. When you breathe in, the scent particles in the air dissolve in the mucus. The smell receptors pick up the information and then pass it on to the olfactory nerve cells, which carry it to the brain where the nerve impulses are interpreted.

If we want to identify a particular smell, we sniff. This carries more scent particles higher up into the nostrils, directly on to the receptors, which creates a stronger response that the brain can interpret more easily.

FACT FILE

Dogs have a larger olfactory bulb, relative to their size, than humans and scientists think that this is because dogs rely on their sense of smell more than we do.

WHY DOESN'T BLOOD FLOW BACKWARDS?

A vein is a blood vessel that carries blood towards the heart. The blood circulates in the body through a system of tubes called blood vessels. The blood in your veins travels quite slowly, and many large veins have valves to stop the blood from draining backwards towards the legs and feet.

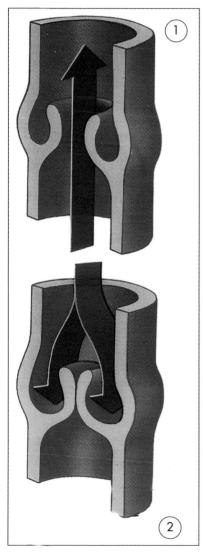

Blood flowing forwards forces the valve flaps to open (1). Blood flowing back forces them to shut (2). The valves in the heart work in exactly the same way.

Blood is also helped along by the arm and leg muscles contracting. That is why, if you stand still for a long period of time, blood can collect in your legs and make them puffy and sore.

FACT FILE

The lymphatic system is one of the body's defences against infection. Harmful particles and bacteria that have entered the body are filtered out by small masses of tissue that lie along the lymphatic vessels. These bean-shaped masses are called lymph nodes.

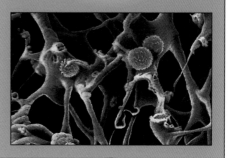

WHERE ARE THE JUGULAR VEINS SITUATED?

The jugular vein is the name of each of four large veins that return blood to the heart from the head and neck. The veins get their name from the Latin word *jugulus*, which means collarbone. There are two jugular veins on each side of the neck, known as the external and internal jugulars. The external jugulars lie close to the surface and carry blood from the outer parts of the head and neck to the heart. The internal jugulars lie further in and carry blood from the deeper tissues of the neck and from the interior of the skull. The internal jugular veins are much larger than the external, and are the ones commonly referred to as jugulars. Opening an internal jugular vein usually proves fatal, because of the rapid loss of blood.

FACT FILE

Whiplash is a term commonly used to describe a type of injury to the neck. This kind of injury results from a sudden blow that throws the head rapidly backward and forward.

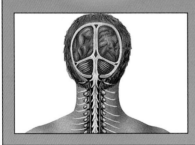

Jugular vein

WHICH BONES FORM THE PELVIS?

Two big, symmetrical hipbones form the pelvis. These bones join in front to form the pubic symphysis. In the back, they form a strong union with the sacrum. Each hipbone in an adult appears to be one solid bone, but it is formed by three bones, the ilium, the ischium and the pubis, that unite as the body matures. The ilium is the broad, flat bone you feel when you rest your hand on your hip. When you sit down, much of your weight rests on the ischium.

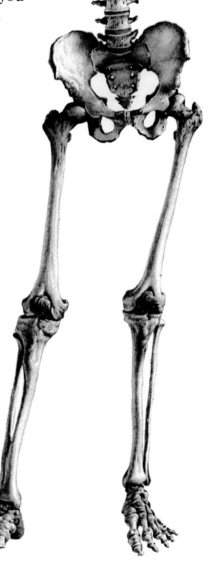

The pelvis is the bony structure that supports the lower abdomen. It surrounds the urinary bladder, the last portion of the large intestine, and, in women, the reproductive organs. A female's pelvis is flatter and broader than a male's and it has a larger central cavity.

FACT FILE

The spinal column joins the pelvis at the sacroiliac joints. The femurs (thigh bones) join the lower part of the pelvis with large ball-and-socket hip joints that allow the legs to move in many directions.

Ball and socket joint

WHAT TRAVELS DOWN THE ALIMENTARY CANAL?

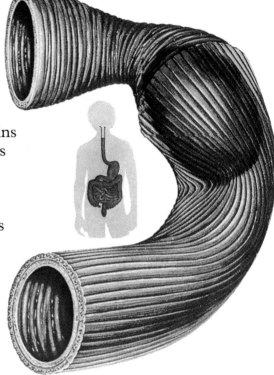

The alimentary canal is a long tube through which food is taken into the body and digested. In human beings, this passage is about 9 metres (30 ft) long. The alimentary canal begins at the mouth, and includes the pharynx, oesophagus, stomach, small and large intestines and rectum.

When a person swallows food, the muscles of the pharynx push the food into the oesophagus. The muscles in the oesophagus walls respond with a wave-like contraction called peristalsis. At the same time, the lower oesophageal sphincter relaxes, allowing the food to pass down to the stomach where digestion begins.

FACT FILE

The human oesophagus is about 25 cm (10 in) long. The length varies greatly in different animals. The oesophagus of fish is short, while that of giraffes is extremely long. Many birds have a saclike part of the oesophagus called the crop for temporary storage of food.

WHAT IS THE AUTONOMIC NERVOUS SYSTEM?

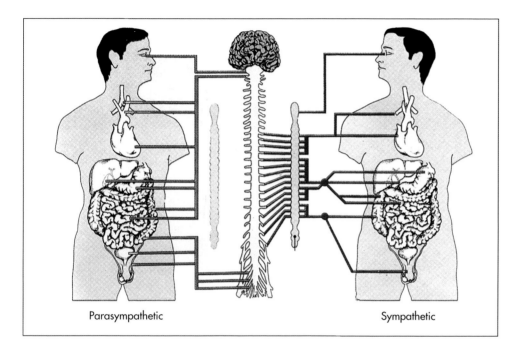

Parasympathetic   Sympathetic

The autonomic nervous system regulates such automatic bodily processes as breathing and digestion without conscious control by the brain. This constant regulation enables the body to maintain a stable internal environment. The autonomic nervous system has two parts, the sympathetic and the parasympathetic system. The parasympathetic nerves tend to make the body calm and relaxed, and slow down processes such as digestion and heartbeat. The sympathetic nerves speed up all these processes and activities, so that the body is ready to spring into action. Between them, these two sets of nerves fine-tune the body's internal conditions.

FACT FILE

The whole of the autonomic system is controlled by an area of the brain called the hypothalamus. This receives information about any variations in your body.

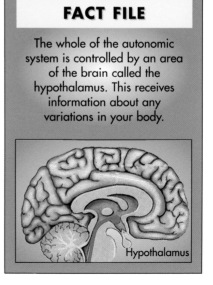

Hypothalamus

157

HOW MANY MUSCLES ARE THERE IN THE HUMAN BODY?

The human body has more than 600 major muscles. About 240 of them have specific names. There are two main types of muscles: (1) skeletal muscles and (2) smooth muscles. A third kind of muscle, called cardiac muscle, has characteristics of both skeletal and smooth muscles. It is found only in the heart.

Skeletal muscles help hold the bones of the skeleton together and give the body shape. They also make the body move. Skeletal muscles make up a large part of the legs, arms, abdomen, chest, neck and face. These muscles vary greatly in size, depending on the type of job they do. For example, eye muscles are small and fairly weak, but the muscles of the thigh are large and strong.

FACT FILE

Cardiac muscle makes up the walls of the heart. When cardiac muscle cells contract, they push blood out of the heart and into the arteries.

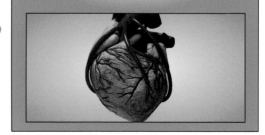

WHERE ARE THE SMOOTH MUSCLES FOUND?

Smooth muscles are found in the walls of the stomach, intestines, blood vessels and bladder. They operate slowly and automatically in a natural, rhythmic pattern of contraction followed by relaxation. In this way, they control various body processes. For example, the steady action of smooth muscles in the stomach and intestines moves food along for digestion. Because they are not under conscious control by the brain, smooth muscles are also known as involuntary muscles. Smooth muscles are stimulated by a special set of nerves that belong to the autonomic nervous system, and by body chemicals.

Cardiac muscle

Smooth muscles

Skeletal muscles

FACT FILE

Muscle cells are excitable because the membrane of each cell is electrically charged. Thus, a muscle cell is said to have electric potential.

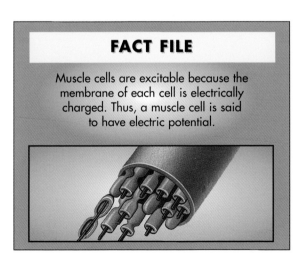

HOW DO THE KIDNEYS WORK?

Human kidneys consist of three layers. These layers are, in order, the cortex on the outside of the organ, the medulla and the pelvis. Blood flows into the medulla through the renal artery. In the medulla and cortex, the renal artery branches into increasingly smaller arteries. Each of these arteries ends in a blood filtration unit called a nephron. Blood flows at high pressure through the capillaries of the Bowman's capsule (1) and only small molecules are forced through the walls (2) into the first part of the nephron (3). The filtrate passes down the proximal tubule, which secretes further metabolites and salts (4) and reabsorbs water, sodium, essential salts, glucose and amino-acids into the blood (5). Unwanted salts, urea and water are left as urine (6).

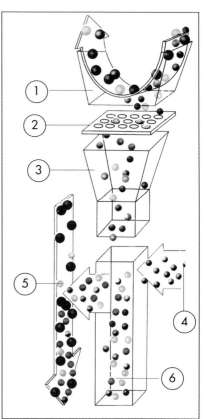

FACT FILE

Two healthy kidneys contain a total of about 2 million nephrons, which filter about 1,900 litres (500 gallons) of blood daily.

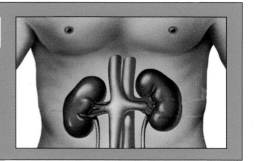

HOW DO THE KIDNEYS CONTROL BLOOD PRESSURE?

The kidneys help maintain the blood pressure of the body by releasing an enzyme called renin. The level of renin in the body depends upon the level of salt, which in turn is controlled by the action of the adrenal hormone, aldosterone, on the tubules. Renin activates another hormone, angiotensin. This has two effects: first it constricts the arterioles and raises the blood pressure; second, it causes the adrenal gland to release aldosterone, making the kidneys retain salt and causing the blood pressure to rise.

The two kidneys perform many vital functions, of which the most important is the production of urine. But in addition to this, the kidneys secrete a hormone called erythropoietin, which controls the production of red blood cells. The kidneys convert vitamin D from an inactive to an active form. The active form is essential for normal bone development.

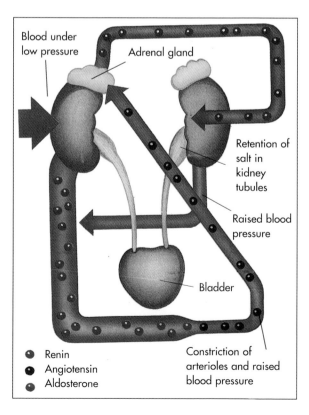

Blood under low pressure

Adrenal gland

Retention of salt in kidney tubules

Raised blood pressure

Bladder

Constriction of arterioles and raised blood pressure

- Renin
- Angiotensin
- Aldosterone

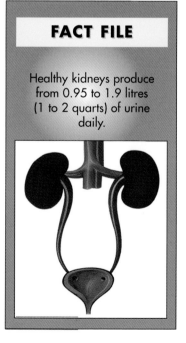

FACT FILE

Healthy kidneys produce from 0.95 to 1.9 litres (1 to 2 quarts) of urine daily.

WHERE DOES THE BODY STORE BILE?

Bile is stored in a small pouch called the gallbladder, a pear-shaped sac that rests on the underside of the right portion of the liver. It can hold about 44 ml (1½ fluid ounces) of bile at one time. The neck of the gallbladder connects with the cystic duct, which enters the hepatic duct, a tube from the liver. Together, these two tubes form the common bile duct.

During digestion, bile flows from the liver through the hepatic duct into the common bile duct and empties into the duodenum, which is the first section of the small intestine. Between meals, the bile is not needed but it continues to flow from the liver into the common bile duct. It is kept out of the duodenum by a small, ringlike muscle called the sphincter of Oddi, which tightens around the opening. The fluid is then forced to flow into the gallbladder, where it is concentrated and stored until it is needed for digestion.

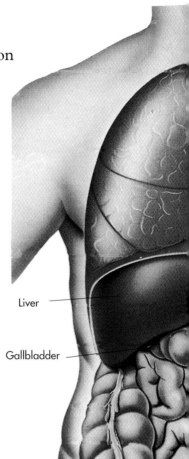

Liver

Gallbladder

FACT FILE

Sometimes the gallbladder becomes filled with hard lumps, on average about the size of a pea. They are made from various substances, chiefly cholesterol and calcium. They can be removed by surgery or smashed into tiny pieces by very high-pitched sound waves called ultrasound.

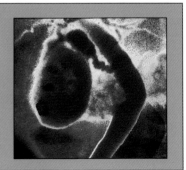

FROM WHERE DOES THE LIVER GET ITS BLOOD?

The liver probably performs more separate tasks than any other organ in the body. Its chief functions are to help the body digest and use food and to help purify the blood of wastes and poisons. The liver has an unusual blood supply system. Like other organs, the liver receives blood containing oxygen from the heart. This blood enters the liver through the hepatic artery. The liver also receives blood filled with nutrients, or digested food particles, from the small intestine. This blood enters the liver through the portal vein. In the liver, the hepatic artery and the portal vein branch into a network of tiny blood vessels that empty into the sinusoids.

The liver cells absorb nutrients and oxygen from the blood as it flows through the sinusoids. They also filter out wastes and poisons. At the same time, they secrete sugar, vitamins, minerals and other substances into the blood. The sinusoids drain into the central veins, which join to form the hepatic vein. Blood leaves the liver through the hepatic vein.

Stomach

Spleen

FACT FILE

The liver plays an essential role in the storage of certain vitamins. The liver stores vitamin A, as well as vitamins D, E and K and those of the B-complex group. It also stores iron and other minerals.

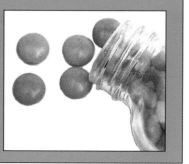

HOW DO DEAF PEOPLE COMMUNICATE?

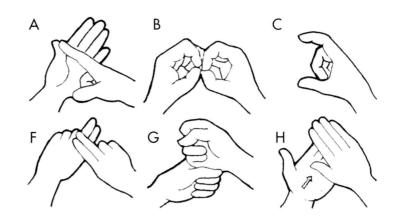

A   B   C

F   G   H

Many people who are deaf or hard of hearing use speech reading and manual communication to help them communicate. Speech reading, also called lip reading, involves understanding what is said by watching the movements of the speaker's mouth, face and body. In manual communication, people talk primarily with their hands.

Manual communication usually involves both finger spelling and sign languages. In finger spelling, a different hand signal represents each letter of the alphabet. In sign languages, hand signals stand for objects and ideas. Sign languages are used throughout the world in the same rich variety as spoken languages. Deaf people use manual communication to converse with people who understand finger spelling and sign language.

FACT FILE

Although deafness poses special challenges, the condition need not hinder achievement in a wide variety of occupations. The German composer Ludwig van Beethoven wrote some of his finest music after he became deaf.

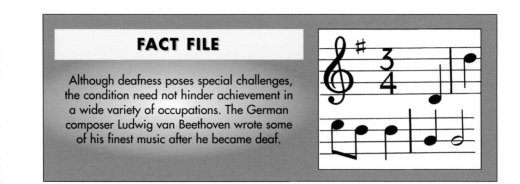

WHAT IS BODY LANGUAGE?

Body language is the series of gestures and movements we make with our face, head, arms, hands and indeed our whole bodies, to signal thoughts and feelings. Head and facial gestures can say a lot about how we feel. How often do you raise your eyebrows when you are surprised, for instance, or nod your head when you say 'yes'? Our body language shows how we feel. People who are tired tend to hunch up and look smaller. People who are excited and happy make big and confident gestures. Whole body gestures, meaning the way we stand or sit, can also communicate a lot. Confident people tend to show they are sure of themselves by standing up straight. A fine example of body language is when two dogs meet. You will see them take up a number of different poses at various times – ears and nose down, tail between legs, ears pricked, teeth bared, or tail up and wagging. It is actions like these that allow dogs to tell each other when they want to fight, to run away, or to make friends.

FACT FILE

People's gestures often mean different things in different countries. In some countries people shake hands when they greet each other, for example, but in other countries people rub noses to say hello or goodbye.

HOW MUCH ENERGY DO WE NEED?

Nutrition is the science that deals with food and how the body uses it. People, like all living things, need food to live. Food supplies the energy for every action we perform, from reading a book to running a race. Food also provides substances that the body needs to build and repair its tissues and to regulate its organs and systems.

The body's need for energy from the diet varies not only with activity, sex, health and climate, but also with age. The size of the figures in the diagram above show the comparative energy requirements from birth to adulthood. Up to two years old, the rapidly growing child needs more than anyone in proportion to size; by old age, when metabolism is slowest, the need is far less.

Water is needed in great amounts because the body consists largely of water. Usually, between 50 and 75 per cent of a person's body weight is made up of water.

FACT FILE

Proteins provide some energy, but more important, they serve as one of the main building materials of the body.

AT WHAT AGE DO WE LEARN TO WALK?

A new-born baby lies with its knees drawn up. It automatically grasps any object that touches its palm and when held upright automatically steps as its feet touch something. It roots and sucks the nipple automatically. These reflexes disappear within a few weeks. At one month old its legs are straighter and by

six weeks it can lift its head. The baby sleeps more often than not, but gradually its eyes focus on objects and at about six weeks it begins to smile. By six months its birth weight is doubled and the child can sit unaided. At eight months the preliminary gurglings of speech are heard and the baby can use its thumb. At about ten months it starts to crawl and its birth weight is trebled.

The first step may be taken at a year old. The first words may be spoken during the next two or three months.

WHAT ARE CHROMOSOMES?

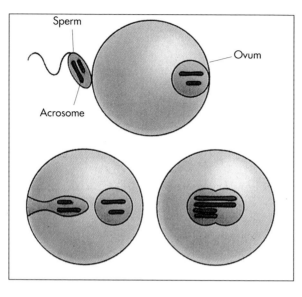

Sperm

Ovum

Acrosome

The moment of conception is the most important stage of sexual reproduction. Fertilization is complete when the chromosomes of the male sperm unite with the chromosomes of the female egg. Chromosomes are threadlike structures that contain genes, the units of heredity that determine each person's unique traits. Most body cells have 46 chromosomes that occur in 23 pairs. However, as each egg or sperm develops, it undergoes a special series of cell divisions called meiosis. As a result, each sperm or egg cell contains only one member of each chromosome pair, or 23 unpaired chromosomes. During fertilization, the chromosomes pair up so that the fertilized egg has the normal number of 46 chromosomes. Only about 100 sperm survive the journey of nearly 24 hours and only one fertilizes the ovum. The sperm's acrosome disappears as it dissolves the membrane of the ovum. The tail and body are shed when the head penetrates to join its 23 chromosomes with those of the ovarian nucleus.

FACT FILE

Special sex chromosomes determine whether the zygote will develop into a boy or a girl. Each body cell contains a pair of sex chromosomes. In females, the two sex chromosomes are identical.

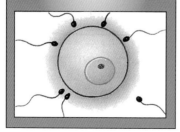

WHAT HAPPENS TO A FERTILIZED EGG?

Morula

A fertilized egg (or zygote) goes through a series of changes before it reaches the uterus. In the uterus, the zygote develops into a form called the embryo, which develops rapidly. The zygote then travels through the fallopian tube toward the uterus. Along the way, the zygote begins to divide rapidly into many cells with no increase in overall size. The resulting cell mass is called a *morula*. By the third or fourth day the morula enters the uterus and the embryo develops from the central cells of the morula. They develop into the placenta, a special organ that enables the embryo to obtain food and oxygen from the mother. After the morula enters the uterus, it continues to divide. At this stage, the ball of cells is called a *blastocyst*. The cells of the blastocyst divide as it

Blastocyst

Trophoblast

floats in the uterus for one or two days. About the fifth or sixth day of pregnancy, the blastocyst becomes attached to the internal surface of the uterus. The outer cells of the blastocyst, called the *trophoblast*, secrete an enzyme that breaks down the lining of the uterus. The trophoblast begins to divide rapidly, invading the uterine tissue. The process of attachment to the uterine wall is called implantation.

FACT FILE

By the 11th day of the pregnancy, the blastocyst is firmly implanted in the uterus. Various structures develop in the uterus to help the embryo grow. These structures include the placenta and certain membranes.

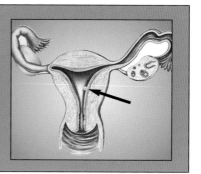

HOW DOES THE BREAST PRODUCE MILK?

Two pituitary hormones are responsible for the production of breast milk: prolactin stimulates the breast to produce milk and oxytocin starts milk flow. The baby's sucking of the nipples also stimulates lactation. A mother's milk is a complete source of food and energy for the baby. It also contains antibodies that protect the infant from many diseases. The breast is an organ specially designed to produce milk to feed a baby.

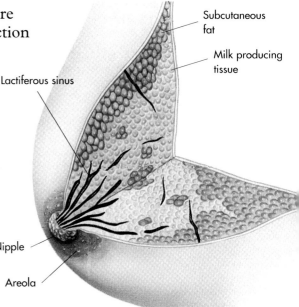

Subcutaneous fat

Milk producing tissue

Lactiferous sinus

Nipple

Areola

FACT FILE

Breast milk is secreted by the lining of the alveoli (below). As the baby feeds, the milk is drawn down the ducts, from where it is sucked out of the nipple.

Human beings have two breasts, but only those of mature females can produce milk.

The breast is composed of 15 to 20 modified sweat glands developing into lobes. The female breast gland develops rapidly at puberty with secreting cells responding to the hormones in the menstrual cycle. During pregnancy the glands become congested and milk is collected in the lactiferous sinuses, which join behind the areola of the nipple. The areola is lubricated by the moist secretion of sebaceous glands.

WHAT DOES THE THYROID GLAND DO?

The thyroid gland is a body organ located in the front of the neck. It has two lobes, one on each side of the trachea (or windpipe). The lobes are connected by a thin band of tissue, while a network of blood vessels surrounds the gland. The thyroid takes iodine from the blood and uses it to make the active hormones thyroxine, also called tetraiodothyronine, and triiodothyronine. An inactive form of thyroid hormones is stored inside the lobes in small chambers called follicles.

Thyroid hormones control the body's cell metabolism. When thyroid hormones are released into the bloodstream, cells increase the rate at which they convert oxygen and nutrients into energy and heat for the body's use. During a child's development, thyroid hormones stimulate an increase in growth rate. Release of thyroid hormones also stimulates mental activity and increases the activity of the other hormone-producing glands.

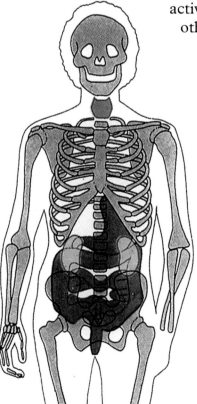

FACT FILE

An underactive thyroid, called hypothyroidism, is a defect that results in the low production of thyroid hormones. This deficiency causes an overall decrease in both physical and mental activity.

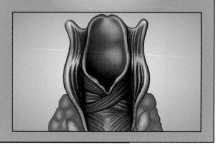

HOW MANY CELLS DOES THE HUMAN BODY HAVE?

FACT FILE

All cells have some things in common, whether they are specialized cells or one-celled organisms. A cell is alive – as alive as you are. It 'breathes', takes in food, and gets rid of wastes. It also grows and reproduces and, in time, it dies.

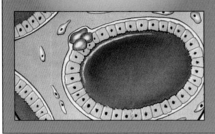

The human body has more than 10 trillion (10,000,000,000,000) cells. A cell is the basic unit of all life and all living things are made up of them.

Most cells are so small they can be seen only with a microscope. It would take about 40,000 of your red blood cells to fill this letter O. It takes millions of cells to make up the skin on the palm of your hand. Some one-celled organisms lead independent lives. Others live in loosely organized groups. As you read these words, for example, nerve cells in your eyes are carrying messages of what you are reading to your brain cells. Muscle cells attached to your eyeballs are moving your eyes across the page.

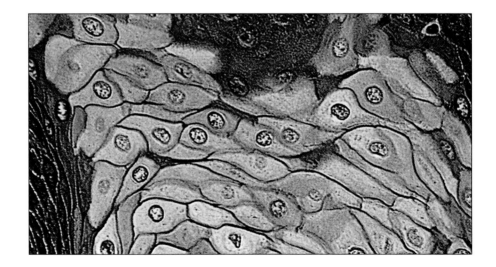

HOW CAN ENZYMES HELP US?

An enzyme is a molecule that speeds up chemical reactions in all living things. Without enzymes, these reactions would occur too slowly or not at all, and no life would be possible. The human body has thousands of kinds of enzymes. Each kind does one specific job. Without enzymes, a person could not breathe, see, move or digest food.

Enzymes have many uses in addition to their natural functions in the body. Manufacturers use enzymes in making a wide variety of products. Some detergents contain enzymes that break down protein or fats that cause stains. Enzymes are also used in the manufacture of antibiotics, beer, bread, cheese, coffee, sugars, vinegar, vitamins and many other products. Physicians use medicines containing enzymes to help clean wounds, dissolve blood clots, relieve certain forms of leukaemia and check allergic reactions to penicillin. Doctors also diagnose some diseases by measuring the amount of various enzymes in blood and other body fluids. Such diseases include anaemia, cancer, leukaemia and heart and liver ailments.

FACT FILE

In the future, enzymes may be widely used to change raw sewage into useful products. Enzymes may also be used to help get rid of spilled oil that harms lakes and oceans. The enzymes would turn the oil into food for sea plants.

SPACE AND

TECHNOLOGY

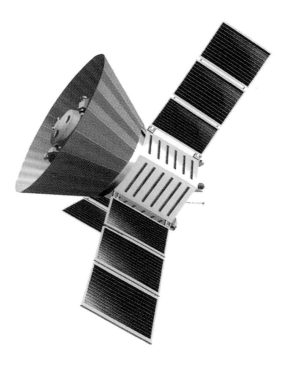

CONTENTS

• •

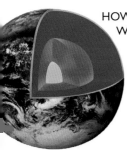

WHEN WAS THE FIRST WEATHER SATELLITE LAUNCHED?

Forty years ago, weather predictions were about as accurate as forecasts of who will win the lottery. In the days before television could warn on a Wednesday of rainy periods at the weekend, weather monitoring was limited to wind, temperature and rainfall gauges aboard aeroplanes, balloons and ships.

All that changed on April 1, 1960 when the US Government launched the first weather satellite, called TIROS 1, into the Earth's orbit from Cape Canaveral, Florida. It paved the way for generations of weather satellites that today help with everything from monitoring crops to tracking the movement of mosquitoes across continents.

FACT FILE

Thanks to the Internet, meteorologists can view high-resolution satellite images of incoming storms, allowing coastal areas enough advance warning to evacuate.

WHAT DO ASTRONAUTS EAT IN SPACE?

FACT FILE

The standard Shuttle menu repeats after seven days. It supplies each crew member with three balanced meals, plus snacks.

Early astronauts found the task of eating in space fairly easy, but found the menu to be limited. They had to endure bite-sized cubes, freeze-dried powders, and semi-liquids stuffed in metal tubes.

With improved packaging came improved food quality and menus. Gemini astronauts had such food choices as prawn cocktail, chicken and vegetables, butterscotch pudding and apple sauce, and were able to select meal combinations themselves.

With improved technology the quality and variety of food increased even further. Apollo astronauts were the first to have hot water, which made rehydrating foods easier and improved the taste of the food. These astronauts were also the first to use the 'spoon bowl', a plastic container that could be opened and its contents eaten with a spoon.

A space kitchen

WHAT TYPE OF TRAINING DOES AN ASTRONAUT NEED?

Candidates for manned spaceflight are carefully screened to meet the highest physical and mental standards, and they undergo rigorous training. As far as is possible, all conditions to be encountered in space are simulated in ground training. Astronauts are trained to function effectively in cramped quarters while wearing restrictive spacesuits. They are accelerated in giant centrifuges to test their reactions during liftoff. They are prepared for the disorientation they will experience in space as a result of weightlessness, and they spend long periods in isolation chambers to test their psychological reactions to solitude. Using trainers and mock-ups of actual spacecraft, astronauts rehearse every exercise from liftoff to recovery, and they prepare for every conceivable malfunction and difficulty.

FACT FILE

In addition to flight training, astronauts are required to have thorough knowledge of all aspects of space science, such as celestial mechanics and rocketry.

WHY DO ASTRONAUTS NEED TO EXERCISE IN SPACE?

Because muscles do not have to fight against gravity in space, they can waste away, which means that astronauts must exercise every day. Conditions in space can be very strange. There is almost no gravity inside a space station, which means that astronauts can float in mid-air and lift heavy objects

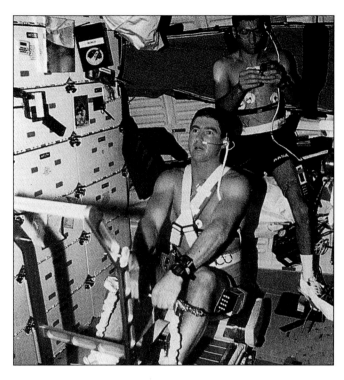

effortlessly. This lack of gravity can be a problem as scientists in space stations have to strap themselves to the walls when they are working to stop themselves from floating away. In addition, there is no proper night and day on a space station. For example, on Mir the sun rises and sets every ninety minutes.

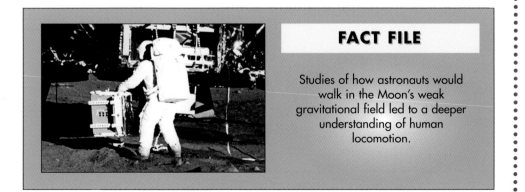

FACT FILE

Studies of how astronauts would walk in the Moon's weak gravitational field led to a deeper understanding of human locomotion.

HOW DO ASTRONAUTS MOVE ABOUT IN SPACE?

FACT FILE

In an emergency, the backpacks would enable tumbling astronauts first to right themselves and then to scurry back to safety at a rate of about 3 m (10 ft) per second.

Astronauts often have to repair components of satellites or space stations. Movement in space can be very difficult and can hamper these tasks. Microgravity means that an astronaut is in danger of floating away or losing a vital tool into outer space. Handles and special footholds, into which feet can be locked, help astronauts move around in space. When they have to fly further away from their Shuttles, astronauts can use special backpacks that have rockets built into them. These backpacks are a little like floating armchairs and are directed by a hand-held device like a joystick. These backpacks are powered by 24 nitrogen gas thrusters.

WHAT ARE SPACE SUITS MADE OF?

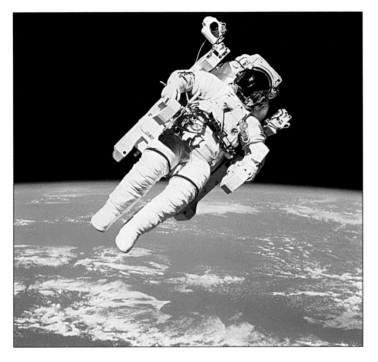

Space suits are made of specially adapted man-made materials, for example, urethane-coated nylon. Designing a spacesuit is a very complex procedure, as the spacesuit needs to give the astronaut complete control and protection; in fact, it needs to act like a miniature spacecraft. It provides everything that an astronaut requires to survive for short periods in space, including oxygen to breathe, water to drink, heating and cooling devices, communication apparatus and toilet facilities. These suits have been developed to withstand the extreme conditions of space.

FACT FILE

The suit maintains a constant pressure by surrounding the body with a kind of balloon. This balloon is full of air, which presses against the body in the same way as the Earth's atmosphere.

HOW DOES A SPACE SHUTTLE LEAVE EARTH?

Like other spacecraft, the shuttle is launched from a vertical position. Liftoff thrust is obtained from the orbiter's three main engines and the boosters. After two minutes the boosters use up all their fuel, separate from the spacecraft are recovered following splashdown with the aid of their attached parachutes. After about eight minutes of flight, the orbiter's main engines shut down, the external tank is then jettisoned and burns up as it re-enters the atmosphere. The orbiter meanwhile enters orbit after a short burn of its two small Orbiting Maneouvering System (OMS) engines. To return to Earth, the orbiter turns around, fires its OMS engines to reduce speed and, after descending through the atmosphere, lands like a glider.

FACT FILE

Following four orbital test flights of the space shuttle *Columbia* between 1981 and 1982, operational flights began in November 1982.

Columbia space shuttle

WHAT IS A GEOSTATIONARY SATELLITE?

There are two types of weather satellites for long- and short-term observations, which together give a complete picture of Earth's weather system.

Geostationary operational environmental satellites take real-time photos of various regions of the Earth to predict floods, hurricanes, thunderstorms and other severe weather patterns as quickly as possible with the help of radar and other ground systems. A polar-orbiting environmental satellite offers a larger, more long-term picture of the environment. Snapping visible and infra-red photos that measure temperature and moisture, these satellites are able to track patterns affecting the weather and climate of the World.

Satellite's view of Earth

FACT FILE

Both sets of satellites also carry search and rescue transmission instruments so that pilots and mariners in distress can relay messages through them for help.

HOW DO SATELLITES MONITOR VOLCANOES?

Scientists can now analyze weather-satellite pictures to keep an eye on 100 dangerous, remote volcanoes along the Pacific Rim in Alaska and Russia. What they are looking for is the excess heat that indicates that a volcano is likely to erupt. The method allows scientists to observe volcanoes when it is too expensive to install earthquake sensors to listen for signs of imminent eruptions.

Only 27 volcanoes in Alaska and Russian Kamchatka are monitored seismically because reaching these remote locations is difficult and costly – long periods of winter darkness render solar-powered monitoring stations useless and the extreme cold makes batteries inefficient. So for the past few years, scientists have routinely examined infra-red images taken by weather satellites.

FACT FILE

The heat-sensing satellites not only help predict eruptions, they also monitor eruptions in progress. Scientists use the pictures to track volcanic ash plumes and recognize lava flows and lava domes.

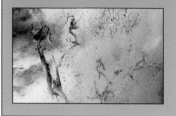

ARE THERE REALLY UFOS?

An unidentified flying object (or UFO) is a light or object in the air that has no obvious explanation. Some people believe UFOs are spaceships from other planets. However, investigators discover ordinary explanations for most UFO sightings, largely because most witnesses are generally reliable individuals. Many reported UFOs are actually bright planets, stars or meteors. People have reported aircraft, missiles, satellites, birds, swarms of insect and weather balloons as UFOs. Unusual weather conditions can also create optical illusions that are reported as UFOs.

Investigators can explain all but a small percentage of UFO reports. The remainder may be due to an unknown phenomenon or merely to limitations in human perception, memory and research. Most scientists believe that there is not enough reliable evidence to connect these sightings with life from other planets.

FACT FILE

Some UFOs are called 'flying saucers'. This term was coined by the press in 1947 to describe a sighting by Kenneth Arnold, a civilian pilot, who reported unknown objects speeding through the air.

HOW MANY COMMUNICATIONS SATELLITES ARE IN ORBIT?

There are hundreds of active communications satellites now in orbit. Communications satellites were originally designed to operate in a passive mode. Instead of actively transmitting radio signals, they served merely to reflect signals that were beamed up to them from transmitting stations on the ground. Signals were reflected in all directions, so they could be picked up by receiving stations around the world. *Echo 1*, an early satellite launched by the United States in 1960, consisted of an aluminized plastic balloon 30 m (100 ft) in diameter. Launched in 1964, *Echo 2* was 41 m (135 ft) in diameter. The capacity of such systems was severely limited by the need for powerful transmitters and large ground antennae.

Morelos-B

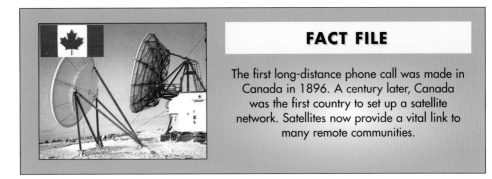

FACT FILE

The first long-distance phone call was made in Canada in 1896. A century later, Canada was the first country to set up a satellite network. Satellites now provide a vital link to many remote communities.

HOW LONG DOES SUNLIGHT TAKE TO REACH EARTH?

From Earth the Sun looks small, because it is so far away. Its average distance from Earth is 150 million km (93 million miles). Light from the Sun takes about eight minutes to reach Earth. This light is still strong enough when it reaches Earth, however, to damage human eyes when viewed directly. The Sun's nearest stellar neighbour, Proxima Centauri, is 4.3 light-years from our Solar System, meaning that light from Proxima Centauri takes 4.3 years to reach the Sun. The Sun is so much closer to Earth than all other stars, that the intense light of the Sun keeps us from seeing any other stars during the daytime.

FACT FILE

Did you know that in northern Scandinavia it doesn't get dark at all in the middle of summer? At the height of summer the tilt of the Earth causes northern countries to get more of the Sun's light.

HOW DOES SPACE RESEARCH HELP US IN DAILY LIFE?

Scientists not only study living organisms in space, but they can also study combustion in microgravity to help design more efficient jet engines. In addition, the study of crystal growth has helped us to build better semiconductors for computers. Everyone has benefitted from the technology that was developed for use in space. Microchips that are used in everything from digital watches to computers were first developed so that lots of equipment could fit into a small spacecraft. Advances such as keyhole surgery, solar power and many ordinary household items such as Velcro and kitchen foil have come about because of science from space technology.

FACT FILE

Professional astronomers today hardly ever use telescopes. Instead, a telescope sends an object's light to a photographic plate or to an electronic light-sensitive computer chip called a charge-coupled device, or CCD. CCDs are about 50 times more sensitive than film, so today's astronomers can record in a minute an image that would have taken about an hour to record on film.

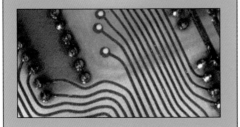

HOW LONG IS A MARTIAN DAY?

FACT FILE

Mars is named after the Roman god of war because it appears fiery red in the Earth's night sky. The surface of Mars is covered by a stony desert that contains lots of iron oxide, giving it its rusty-red appearance.

The Martian day, or the time it takes Mars to rotate once on its axis, is about a half an hour longer than an Earth day. Its year, or the time it takes to revolve once around the Sun, is about two Earth years long.

Mars is a relatively small planet, about half the diameter of the Earth and about one-tenth of the Earth's mass. Because of the relative movements of the Earth and Mars around the Sun, Mars appears to move backwards in the sky for a short time when the two planets are closest.

WHICH PLANET IS CALLED THE MORNING STAR?

Except for the Sun and the Moon, Venus is the brightest object in the sky. The planet is called the 'morning star' when it appears in the east at sunrise, and the 'evening star' when it is in the west at sunset. In ancient times the evening star was called *Hesperus* and the morning star *Phosphorus* or *Lucifer*. Because of the distances of the orbits of Venus and Earth from the Sun, Venus is never visible more than three hours before sunrise or three hours after sunset. Venus's complete cloud cover and deep atmosphere make it difficult to study from Earth, and most of our knowledge of the planet has been obtained through the use of space vehicles, particularly those carrying probes that descend through the atmosphere.

FACT FILE

The powerful radar aboard the *Magellan* spacecraft has revealed huge active volcanoes, large solidified lava flows and a vast array of meteorite craters on the surface of Venus.

WHICH PLANET HAS THE GREATEST TEMPERATURE RANGE?

FACT FILE

Mercury has a large iron core which is between 1,800 and 1,900 km (1,118 and 1,181 miles) thick. The outer shell is about 500 km (311 miles) thick. The planet Mercury has no satellites.

Mercury is only about one-third the size of the Earth. It is smaller than any other planet except Pluto. Mercury is very close to the Sun and has no substantial atmosphere. These factors contribute to the fact that the surface of Mercury has the greatest temperature range of any planet or natural satellite in our solar system. The surface temperature on the side of Mercury closest to the Sun reaches 427°C (800°F), a temperature hot enough to melt tin. On the side facing away from the Sun, or the night side, the temperature drops to -183°C (297°F). Mercury's atmosphere is very thin and is composed of helium and sodium. The surface of Mercury has been shaped by three processes: impact cratering where large objects struck the surface resulting in crater formation, volcanism where lava flooded the surface, and tectonic activity where the planet's crust moved in order to adjust to the planetary cooling and contracting.

HOW MANY PARTS DOES THE EARTH CONSIST OF?

The Earth consists of five parts: the first, the atmosphere, is gaseous; the second, the hydrosphere, is liquid; the third, fourth and fifth, the lithosphere, mantle and core, are largely solid. The atmosphere is the gaseous envelope that surrounds the solid body of the planet. Although it has a thickness of more than 1,100 km (700 miles), about half its mass is concentrated in the lower 5.6 km (3.5 miles). The lithosphere, consisting mainly of the cold, rigid, rocky crust of the Earth, extends to a depth of 100 km (60 miles). The hydrosphere is the layer of water that, in the form of the oceans, covers roughly 70.8 per cent of the surface of the Earth. The mantle and core are the heavy interior of the Earth, making up most of the Earth's mass.

FACT FILE

The Earth's inner core is made up mostly of iron and nickel. It is 1,370 km (850 miles) deep and is thought to have a temperature of around 4,500°C (8,132°F).

WHAT IS THE PANGAEA?

Some 225 million years ago all the world's land masses were joined together into one supercontinent, the Pangaea, surrounded by a single universal sea, the Panthalassa. Through the upheavals that we have since come to know as plate tectonics, the shifting of the Earth's crust tore the supercontinent apart sometime during the middle of the Mesozoic period and large bodies of land drifted across the surface of the Earth ultimately to become our present-day continents. It is now believed that the several moving plates of the Earth's crust were formed by volcanic activity. The clues to the movement of the Earth's surface can be found on the present-day continents in rocks, fossils and structures more than about 200 million years old.

FACT FILE

As a result of the Earth's movement, certain species of terrestrial mammals became isolated in Antarctica, South America, Africa and Australia. It was thousands of years before volcanic eruption would reunite South and North America in a land bridge.

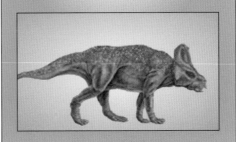

WHAT IS ON THE FAR SIDE OF THE MOON?

The side of the Moon not visible from the Earth is called the far side. One of the discoveries of the first Lunar orbiters is that the far side has a very different appearance than the near side. In particular, there are almost no maria on the far side, but quite a large number of meteor impact craters. The maria (which comprise about 16 per cent of the Moon's surface) are huge impact craters that were later flooded by molten lava. Very little knowledge is known about this side of the Moon.

The face of the Moon closest to us is called the near side. It is divided into light areas called the Lunar Highlands and darker areas called maria. Most of the surface is covered with regolith, which is a mixture of fine dust and rocky debris produced by meteor impacts. For some unknown reason, the maria are concentrated on the near side.

FACT FILE

Mountain ranges, thousands of metres high, form the walls of huge craters on the Moon's surface. Craters discovered on the near side of the Moon have been named after famous people.

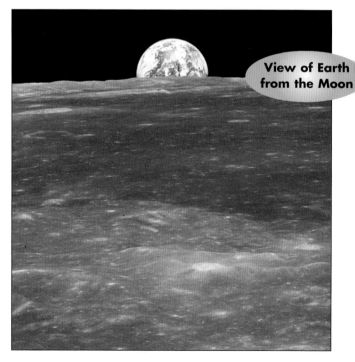

View of Earth from the Moon

WHY DOES THE MOON APPEAR TO CHANGE SHAPE?

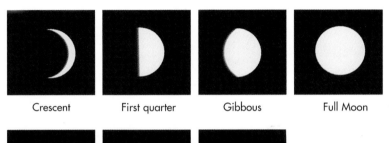

| Crescent | First quarter | Gibbous | Full Moon |

| Gibbous | Last quarter | Crescent |

Each month it seems as though the Moon changes shape. Of course, that is not really the case. Only the part of the Moon that is both turned towards the Earth and lit by the Sun is visible from Earth. The Moon orbits the Earth once every 27.3 days, a lunar month. As the Moon also takes exactly 27.3 days to turn on its axis, the same side of the Moon is always turned towards the Earth. The amount of the Moon that can be seen changes as the Moon's position changes. It is this change in the amount of the Moon's face which we can see from Earth, that makes the Moon look as though it is changing shape. Our word 'month' comes from 'moon', although our calendar months are no longer linked to the phases of the Moon.

FACT FILE

The Moon is close enough to us to have a tremendous effect on conditions on Earth. It is the pull of the Moon's gravity that causes the tides in the seas.

WHAT IS A DIFFUSE NEBULA?

Nebulae, which are clouds of dust and gas, come in many diferent shapes and sizes. Diffuse nebulae are extremely large structures, often many light-years wide, that have no definite outline and a sketchy, cloud-like appearance. They are either luminous or dark. Diffuse nebulae shine as a result of the light of adjacent stars. They include some of the most striking objects in the sky, such as the Great Nebula in Orion. There are known to be many thousands of luminous nebulas in our solar system.

FACT FILE

Dark nebulae appear dark because there are no nearby stars to light them. They can be spotted because they blot out the light from more distant stars.

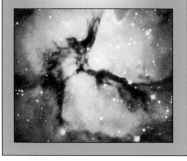

Orion nebula

WHAT IS THE KUIPER BELT?

An astronomer named Gerard Kuiper suggested that beyond Neptune lay a belt of celestial bodies made up from rock and ice. Astronomers now think that there may be as many as 100,000 large, comet-like objects in the Kuiper Belt, including the planet Pluto. The icy bodies in the Kuiper Belt are called minor members, or 'Plutinos' because they act like little Plutos and are very difficult to spot from Earth, even with the most powerful telescopes. If all the objects in the Kuiper Belt joined together, they would form a planet the size of Earth.

FACT FILE

An object in space will be pulled into a spherical shape if its gravitational force is powerful enough. Because the objects in the Kuiper Belt do not have powerful gravitational pulls, they come in all sorts of shapes and sizes.

WHICH PLANET IS ALWAYS DARK AND COLD?

On Pluto it is always dark and cold, even in the middle of the day. This is because the Sun appears 1,000 times fainter from the surface of Pluto than it does from Earth, little more than a faint star. In summer, Pluto has a slight atmosphere because the surface warms up sufficiently to melt some of its ice, turning it to gas. As Pluto moves away from the Sun, the gas freezes and becomes ice once more. This means that in winter, Pluto's weather doesn't just become worse, it completely disappears.

FACT FILE

Little is known about Pluto's atmosphere, but it probably consists primarily of nitrogen with some carbon monoxide and methane.

WHICH IS PLUTO'S COMPANION MOON?

In 1978 Pluto was found to have a companion moon, which scientists named Charon. The moon is one-third the size of Pluto, making it the biggest moon in comparison to its parent planet in the entire Solar System. They are only 20,000 km (12,430 miles) apart, and are caught in a gravitational headlock, forming what scientists call a dual planet system. Nobody knows how Pluto managed to adopt so large a moon. Some believe Charon is made from ice chipped off Pluto by a collision.

FACT FILE

Pluto takes 248 years to orbit the Sun. Amazingly, this means that not even half a year has elapsed on the planet since its discovery in 1930! Another strange feature about Pluto is that it rotates in the opposite direction from most of the other planets.

WHICH IS THE LARGEST TELESCOPE IN THE WORLD?

Two identical telescopes called Keck I and Keck II are the largest reflecting telescopes in the world. Each has a segmented mirror 10 m (33 feet) in diameter. The telescopes are on Mauna Kea, a mountain in Hawaii.

The telescope in an optical observatory which stands under a large dome with shutters. The dome and the shutters protect the telescope from the weather. Motors and precision gears keep the telescope pointed in the desired direction as the Earth rotates. Observatories use two principal kinds of optical telescopes – reflecting telescopes and refracting telescopes. Reflecting telescopes use a curved mirror or a set of such mirrors to focus light, and refracting telescopes use a system of lenses.

FACT FILE

Refracting telescopes need thick lenses for high magnification. The refracting telescope at the Yerkes Observatory in Williams Bay, Wisconsin, is the world's largest lens. It measures 102 cm (40 in) in diameter.

WHO BUILT THE FIRST WORKING ROCKET?

According to historians, the Chinese built the first working rockets. They were also the first to use them for military purposes. In AD 1232, some ingenious military leader used arrows powered by small gunpowder rockets to successfully defend the city of K'ai-Fung-Foo against the invading Mongols.

During this time one Chinese official hit on the idea of using rockets to propel a man through the air. It was in about 1500 that Wan Hu fastened two kites together with a chair in between. He then tied a series of military rockets to the kites and asked a group of coolies to light the rockets. Not wanting to miss out on the chance for fame, Wan Hu decided to be his own test pilot. According to reports, he sat in the chair and gave the order to light the rockets. There was a lot of noise and a great burst of flame and smoke, which blocked everyone's vision. When the smoke cleared, Wan Hu was gone!

FACT FILE

In 1931 Johannes Winkler launched his HW-1 rocket. It went 1.9 metres (2 yards) into the air, turned over and fell back to the ground.

HOW DID WE BENEFIT FROM THE DISCOVERY OF INFRA-RED?

Sir Frederick William Herschel (1738–1822) was born in Germany, and became well known both as a musician and an astronomer. Herschel's experiments with light proved to be important, not only because they led to the discovery of infra-red, but also because it was the first time that someone showed that there were forms of light no visible to us.

Today, infra-red technology has many exciting and useful applications. In the field of infra-red astronomy, new and fascinating discoveries are being made about the Universe. Medical infra-red imaging is a very useful diagnostic tool. Infra-red cameras are used for police and security work as well as in fire fighting and in the military. Infra-red imaging is used to detect heat loss in buildings and in testing electronic systems. Infra-red satellites have been used to monitor the Earth's weather, to study vegetation patterns, and to study geology and ocean temperatures.

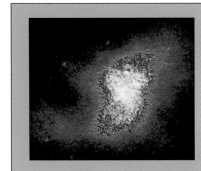

FACT FILE

Ultraviolet and X-ray astronomy are radiation sources of a higher energy level than infra red and are best observed by telescopes orbiting Earth's atmosphere. Ultraviolet astronomy is used to track down the hottest stars.

WHAT ARE MAGELLANIC CLOUDS?

Magellanic Clouds are two galaxies visible in the Southern Hemisphere as small, hazy patches of light. They are the galaxies closest to the Milky Way, the galaxy that contains the Sun, the Earth and the rest of our Solar System. Astronomers classify the Magellanic Clouds as irregular galaxies because the

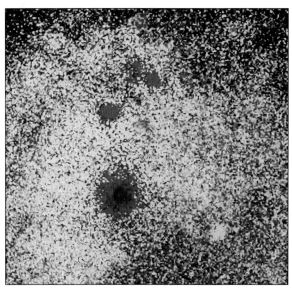

distribution of the stars within them does not follow a particular pattern. The Magellanic Clouds contain billions of stars, but individual stars can be distinguished only by using the most powerful telescopes. As a result, the galaxies appear cloudy to the naked eye. The Magellanic Clouds also contain a huge quantity of gas. New stars are constantly forming from this gas, which is composed mainly of hydrogen. In addition, much of the light from the Magellanic Clouds comes from young, extremely luminous, hot blue stars that are surrounded by glowing clouds of this gas.

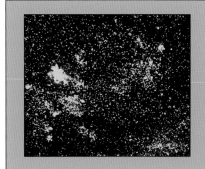

FACT FILE

Magellanic Clouds were first recorded in the early 16th century during the world's first circumnavigation by the Portuguese explorer Ferdinand Magellan, after whom they were named.

HOW DO ASTRONAUTS TRAVEL ON THE MOON'S SURFACE?

In later Apollo missions, astronauts took the Lunar Rover or Moon Buggy with them. This enabled them to explore further than had been possible before. Equipment on board the buggy included a television camera and a satellite dish so that pictures could be sent back to Earth. To avoid damage from the rough surface of the Moon, the tyres were solid. Steering was controlled by a small hand control rather than a wheel. The Lunar Rover was powered by a battery, and its top speed was just under 20 kph (12 mph). It also carried tool kits and bags for geological samples.

FACT FILE

Altogether there have been six Apollo missions to the Moon, during which 12 astronauts have explored its conditions and composition. They have tested the soil to determine what the Moon is made from and also measured Moonquakes.

WHY WILL FOOTPRINTS STAY ON THE MOON FOREVER?

The footprints left by Apollo astronauts will last for centuries because there is no wind on the Moon. The flag the Americans left on the Moon is held out by a metal bar because there is no wind to make it fly.

The Moon does not possess any atmosphere, so there is no weather as we are used to on Earth. Because there is no atmosphere to trap heat, the temperatures on the Moon vary dramatically over the course of a day, from 100°C at noon to -173°C at night. The Moon has no rain or earthquakes to wear away or break down the craters, so they have remained the same for millions of years.

The Moon does not produce its own light, but it looks bright because it reflects light from the Sun. Think of the Sun as a light bulb, and the Moon as a mirror, reflecting light from the light bulb. The lunar phase changes as the Moon orbits the Earth and different portions of its surface are illuminated by the Sun.

FACT FILE

Sometimes the Moon appears orange. This occurs when there is a lot of dust, smoke or pollution in the atmosphere. The size of those particles will determine what you see. Sometimes the Moon will look red, orange . . . even blue.

WHAT IS A SOLAR WIND?

Charged particles are constantly being given off by the Sun. They are known as the Solar Wind and are strongest when the sunspot activity is at its height. When the Solar Wind reaches the Earth's magnetic field, the charged particles interact with gases in the Earth's atmosphere 10 km (6 miles) above the surface. This interaction causes the particles to send out light, which is seen from Earth as an amazing lightshow, best visible from within the Arctic and Antarctic Circles. In the northern hemisphere this is known as the *aurora borealis*, and in the southern hemisphere as the *aurora australis*.

FACT FILE

Darker areas on the surface of the Sun are called sunspots. These areas of cooler gas occur when the Sun's magnetic field blocks the flow of heat from the core.

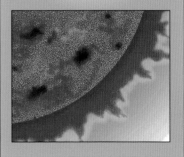

WHERE WOULD YOU SEE BAILEY'S BEADS?

A total eclipse of the Sun can be quite frightening, turning day into night in a spectacular fashion. However, as the Moon appears to eat the Sun, some incredibly beautiful 'special effects' take place. Just before the Sun disappears, a brilliant bright spot can be seen on the edge of the Moon, a little like a diamond on a ring. This is caused by the last fingers of the Sun's light filtering through valleys and mountain ranges on the Moon. Sometimes the bright spot can appear as an arc of glowing pearls, an effect known as Bailey's Beads.

FACT FILE

It is important never to look directly at the Sun, even during an eclipse. This can cause blindness.

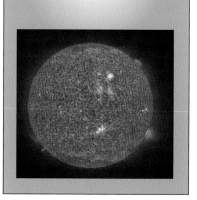